POLITICAL REALITIES
Edited on behalf of the Politics Association
by Bernard Crick and Derek Heat~

GW00720565

LOCAL GOVERNMENT AND POLITICS

POLITICAL REALITIES
Edited on behalf of the Politics Association
by Bernard Crick and Derek Heater

POLITICAL REALITIES

Local Government and Politics

Martin Cross and David Mallen

Longman

LONGMAN GROUP LIMITED
London
Associated Companies branches and representatives
throughout the world

First published in 1978

ISBN 0 582 36611 9 (cased)
ISBN 0 582 36622 4 (paper)
Printed in Hong Kong by Wing Tai Cheung Printing Co. Ltd.

Contents

Acknowledgements

Mr. Royston Greenwood *et al* for Fig. 2 from 'Contingency Theory and the Organisation of Local Authorities' Hinings, Greenwood, Ranson, which appeared in the Journal *Public Administration* (Summer 1975); Her Majesty's Stationery Office for extracts from Vols. I and III of the *Report of the Royal Commission on Local Government in England,* Cmnd 4040 and Cmnd 4040-II, also a brief extract and Appendix J of the Bains Report from *The New Local Authorities: Management and Structure* reproduced with the permission of the Controller of Her Majesty's Stationery Office.

Political Realities:
the nature of the series

A great need is felt for short books which can supplement or even replace textbooks and which can deal in an objective but realistic way with problems that arouse political controversy. The series aims to break from a purely descriptive and institutional approach to one that will show how and why there are different interpretations both of how things work and how they ought to work. Too often in the past "British Constitution" has been taught quite apart from any knowledge of the actual political conflicts which institutions strive to contain. So the Politics Association sponsors this new series because it believes that a specifically civic education is an essential part of any liberal or general education, but that respect for political rules and an active citizenship can only be encouraged by helping pupils, students and young voters to discover what the main objects are of political controversy, the varying views about the nature of the constitution – themselves often highly political – and what the most widely canvassed alternative policies are in their society. From such a realistic appreciation of differences and conflicts reasoning can then follow about the common processes of containing or resolving them peacefully.

The specific topics chosen are based on an analysis of the main elements in existing A level syllabuses, and the manner in which they are treated is based on the conviction of the editors that almost every examination board is moving, slowly but surely, away from a concentration on constitutional rules and towards a more difficult but important concept of a realistic political education or the enhancement of political literacy.

This approach has, of course, been common enough in the universites for many years. Quite apart from its civic importance, the teaching of politics in schools has tended to lag behind university practice and expectations. So the editors have aimed to draw on the most up-to-date academic knowledge, with some of the books being written by university teachers, some by secondary or further education teachers, but each aware of the skills and knowledge of the other.

The Politics Association and the editors are conscious of the great importance of other levels of education, and are actively pursuing studies and projects of curriculum development in several directions, particularly towards CSE needs; but it was decided to begin with A level and new developments in sixth form courses precisely because of the great overlap here between teaching in secondary school and further education colleges, whether specifically for examinations or not; indeed most of the books will be equally useful for general studies.

Bernard Crick
Derek Heater

Preface

This volume in the *Political Realities* series differs from other books currently available on the topic of local government in a number of ways. It aims to switch the emphasis in local government studies away from the legal and institutional approach towards a more realistic approach which emphasises the political nature of local decision-making, and which highlights the significant issues in local politics. The first chapter therefore considers the arguments about the nature of local government which have resulted in the present system. The second chapter is devoted specifically to the issues involved in the devolution of power from Westminster, and the role of 'intermediate' governments in the United Kingdom. Thirdly, local finance is examined in its political context; a case-study approach is used to analyse local financial procedures. The remaining chapters are concerned with the people and groups involved in local government, and the relationships between them. A particular effort is made to set new forms of local authority organisation and management in a political context. It is hoped that this book will help teachers and students to realise that political concepts can be approached through a study of the local political system just as well as, if not better than, by a study of the national system.

It should be emphasised that this short book does not attempt to include all the institutional material on local government found in the more conventional textbook. Suggestions for further reading are given for each chapter, but, to save repetition, the two most thorough, conventional texts are mentioned here:

P.W. Jackson, *Local Government,* 3rd Edition, Butterworths,

1976; and P.G. Richards, *The Reformed Local Government System,* Allen and Unwin, 1973.

Our thanks are due to our colleagues in local politics – officers, party members, councillors – who have taught us much, in some cases unintentionally; particularly to David Thompson, Chief Executive of Lewes District Council, for allowing us to use extracts from his diary on pages 101-103; to Frances King, who typed our manuscripts; and most of all to our wives and families for their exceptional patience.

Introduction

The extent to which we are governed locally – or why there are government organisations operating at sub-national level – may not be fully realised, even by the readers of this book. A few minutes' thought on how a typical day, or week, is spent will soon show the very considerable extent to which local government and local administration impinge on our everyday life. Water, sewerage, roads, buses, schools, colleges, playing fields, libraries, parks, police, street lighting, theatres, hospitals: these are but a few of the services we use regularly that are provided by bodies operating at a more local level than the United Kingdom Government. Some of these services are provided by local government, by which is meant democratically elected councils; others are provided by nominated bodies, such as Water Authorities or Health Authorities, which can be described as local administration rather than local government.

Should services be provided by local governments rather than local administrations? Answers to that question recur throughout this book, but a brief rehearsal of the main points is needed before the structure of local government can be sensibly examined. First of all, the needs of different parts of the country vary: what seems important to the inhabitants of Skegness may not seem so important to the inhabitants of Swansea. Perhaps our system of government should enable those varying needs to be recognised in the provision of services to those different groups of people. Secondly, certain services are local in kind. The state of repair of pavements or road surfaces in a residential side road is of no concern to the national government. Thirdly, a theory of democratic involvement would suggest that people should be able to influence decisions on those matters that affect them most closely. Thus, local residents would expect to have a larger say in whether their community should build a community centre than in whether the British Army should be doubled in size – a decision in which the residents of the whole country are involved.

There is therefore a case for local government. At the same time, however, there are factors militating against. It may be more economical, more efficient in terms of staff and buildings, to centralise; there may be pressure for uniform standards to be achieved throughout the country. For many services, too, the question of the appropriate local area is a matter of controversy. In education for instance – should a school be seen as a matter of concern only for those living in its catchment area, or should it be seen as forming a part of a pattern of education over a much wider area, or should it be seen as simply an element in the national provision? How questions of this sort are answered, or have been answered in the past, will determine the distribution of functions between central government, local governments and local administrations.

1 The structure of local government

'Without doubt the opportunities for local authorities to take the vital decisions that affect their areas are more exciting now than at any other time. The Government are determined to return power to those people who should exercise decisions locally, and to ensure that local government is given every opportunity to take that initiative and responsibility effectively, speedily and with vigour.'

With this cry of faith in the potential of a vigorous local government system to play to the full its role within the democratic life of this country, the Conservative Government of 1971 launched its programme of local government reform which was to see the structure fundamentally change in England and Wales in 1974 and in Scotland in 1975. By the summer of 1975 the people to whom the power had been returned were being admonished by the Secretary of State for the Environment who told them that 'the party is over'. In part, this reflected the, by now Labour, Government's concern that the problem of inflation was not being faced realistically (as the Government saw it) by local authorities, but its very tone suggested that the relationship between the Government and local authorities was strained and that the new era of local government had, at best, got off to a poor start and, at worst, had ended after the first false dawn. Could it be that the faith expressed failed to survive its first critical test − despite the quarter of a century of debate on reform? Is the new system going to work any better than the old?

Historical background

The structure of the old system was created at the end of the nineteenth century with the passing of the Local Government Acts of 1888 and 1894. They set out to do two things: to separate town

1

from country and, in the country areas, to create two levels of Authority. (See Table 1.1) This second aim reinforced the first by creating at the local level, within counties, urban districts and non-county boroughs for the towns and rural districts for the country. The legislators were determined that the problems of the rapidly growing urban areas should be seen as quite distinct from those of the rural areas which surrounded them. No recognition was given to the relationship which was bound to develop as the better-off workers within the urban areas moved to the country areas to live. Thus, the Acts contained the seeds of their own destruction – though it must be acknowledged that they were a long time a-dying.

When the original Local Government Bill was presented in 1888, it proposed that there should be ten county boroughs – urban authorities equal in status to counties: Birmingham, Bradford, Bristol, Hull, Leeds, Liverpool, Manchester, Newcastle, Nottingham and Sheffield. All had a population of over 150,000. There was considerable pressure from M.P.s representing urban areas to grant county borough status, and with it independence from 'county rule', to their areas, and the Government made a series of concessions which culminated in a general concession that the minimum size of a county borough should be, not 150,000, but 50,000. The number of towns and cities qualifying increased from the original ten to fifty-nine. The 1888 Act also allowed that any urban area which at some future time reached the required size, could apply for county borough status. Thus, within a year of the passing of the Act, Oxford became a county borough and by 1927 a further twenty-one county boroughs were created (and two were lost: Hanley into Stoke and Devonport into Plymouth). The 1888 Act also allowed for the county boroughs to expand their boundaries. Objections to proposals by the county boroughs or the President of the Local Government Board for a revision of boundaries were possible, but during the first thirty-five years of the life of the Act do not seem to have been accepted very frequently, and in that period there were over a hundred extensions involving 1,700,000 people.

Thus, the counties lost ground to the county boroughs fairly rapidly until the mid-twenties when, as a result of the concern being expressed by the counties at the loss of territory and population, and rateable value, the Government set up a Royal Commission under

Table 1.1. *The structure of local government before 1974*

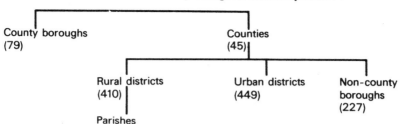

Notes:

1 There were 124 first-tier authorities (counties and county boroughs) and 1,086 second-tier authorities (county districts).
2 County boroughs were responsible for all services; in counties, some functions were at first-tier level, others at second-tier.
3 Sizes of authorities: their population varied enormously:

	Biggest	*Smallest*
County borough	1,074,940	32,790
County	2,428,040	29,680
Rural District	86,390	1,490
Urban District	123,230	1,700
Non-county borough	100,470	1,630

4 The contrast in size of authorities is even greater if looked at by function: e.g. (a) The smallest housing authority, Tintwistle Rural District, had a population of 1,490; the biggest, Birmingham, 1,074,940. (b) The area of the smallest planning authority, Bootle, was 3,300 acres; of the biggest, Devon, 1,612, 373 acres.

Source: *Royal Commission on Local Government in England* (The Redcliffe-Maud Report) Volume 1.

the chairmanship of Lord Onslow. On the recommendations of the Commission, an Act was passed in 1926 which made it more difficult (though not impossible) for county boroughs to expand, and lifted the minimum qualifying population for a new county borough to 75,000. The Act was successful in its efforts to prevent new county boroughs being created at the previous rate. None at all were created between 1927 and 1958 (though, in part, this was due to a wartime moratorium and, in part, to the efforts of the post-war Local Government Boundary Commission to prevent further piecemeal changes). It was also successful in its other aim because whilst the county boroughs continued to acquire new land, usually the population transfer was small and the loss of population suffered by the counties fell to about 10,000 per year. In 1958 an Act was passed which provided for a Local Government Commission whose task it was to review the organisation of local government throughout England, outside London, and make recommendations for change. As a result of its recommendations three new county boroughs (Luton, Solihull and Torbay) were created, some major changes in others (particularly Warley and Teesside) were effected and many others were in the pipeline which were stopped only by the appointment of another Royal Commission under the chairmanship of Lord Redcliffe-Maud.

One thing emerges clearly from this brief summary of the recent development of local government: that there was no philosophy of the role of local government. Unlike other countries, such as the United States and Germany where careful consideration was given to the functions and relationships of the different levels of government, local government in Britain, like Topsy, 'just growed'. The Acts of 1888 and 1894 had tried to rationalise the organisation of a number of functions being carried out at local level. When the counties had been given the task in 1856 of organising police forces, the J.P.s in Quarter Session became the police authority and they also assumed some control over licensing public houses, and slaughter, controlled the provision of asylums, and had powers to inspect food. These powers were transferred in 1888 to the new county and county borough councils, but the J.P.s shared control of the police. The next stage, in 1894, was to create a second level to take over the role of some of the other 'ad hoc' bodies which had been created: in particular, the urban districts and rural districts took over the powers of the old Sanitary Authorities, and the rural district councils became the Poor Law Guardians.

And yet, despite these attempts to rationalise, there was no concept of 'appropriate size' of each authority, nor of what resources would be appropriate. We have seen how the minimum size of county boroughs was changed from 150,000 to 50,000 (and even that was not strictly abided by: Canterbury, Chester, Worcester and Burton-on-Trent all had fewer citizens but were accorded county borough status). We have also seen that county boroughs were able to acquire land from the counties, sometimes at a very significant rate: Coventry, for example, expanded fourteen-fold and several other authorities increased five-fold and more. Urban areas could suddenly be plucked from the county structures. In any case, the county areas were, for the most part, based on the old shires and varied enormously in size and population.

Nor was it only a question of the size and relationships of the local authorities. Their functions also changed considerably with the passing of time. The 1902 Education Act abolished the school boards and made county and county borough councils responsible for primary and secondary education. Since that time they have developed considerable roles in the provision of special education for children with physical or mental disabilities; in further education including technical education; in higher education by the provision of Colleges of Education and Polytechnics. From their responsibilities in health and sanitation, the authorities have developed their role as providers of housing, which again has developed from a straight-forward role as developers and landlords of housing for families to a role which includes supporting and guiding housing associations, improving existing properties and lending money to local citizens wishing to buy a house within the area. In almost all other fields similar patterns can be seen: the beginning and development of public transport, involvement in various areas of social support such as child and old people's welfare, and support to citizens under various forms of stress. At times, provision being made by local authorities was transferred to central government agencies. Certain health functions and the relief of poverty, for example, were transferred with the development of the Welfare State. In each case, the emphasis in deciding the role of local government was how to rationalise a particular service which had developed rather than to try to place local government in a context of national government. Much less was there any attempt to develop a model of democratic control of public services.

It was this very lack of a philosophy of local government which, at least in part, allowed the old structure to survive as long as it did. It had been created by a society which paid scant regard to the public provision of personal services and in an era when most people could scarcely have conceived the explosion of knowledge which was to occur in the twentieth century affecting, as it is doing, every aspect of our lives. It was created to emphasise the separation of town and country, whilst all the pressures of twentieth-century society were to emphasise the inter-relationship of the two. However, because the services were being provided tolerably well, if perhaps in a somewhat uncoordinated way, the demand for change, although persistent, never became irresistible. Nor did there ever seem likely to be a breakdown in the provision of services such as would force a government, of no matter what political persuasion, to make the matter of local government reform a top priority in its legislative programme.

Reorganisation

Why should there be any reluctance at all? Even if not a top priority, surely governments could recognise that the system needed rationalising at least and perhaps even completely recasting? The answer can only be that neither major party wished to alienate its supporters and any reform would perforce do just that. For a start, there was a deep division between the County Councils Association on the one hand and the Association of Municipal Corporations on the other about the basic question of whether a system of unitary authorities was better than a two-level system. Labour had more members in the AMC and the Conservatives more supporters in the CCA. It is not without significance that the Labour Government in its White Paper supported the unitary authority as the basic unit of local government whilst the Conservative Government, in its White Paper and subsequent legislation, lent its support to the two-level system of local government. But, both parties had significant numbers of supporters in each camp and would be unable to avoid offending some supporters. There would also be supporters of whichever government took the decision who would be deeply offended by the act of consigning to oblivion the authority which they had served, often over many years. Add to this the fact that the number of councillors would almost certainly drop (thus reducing the number of party members who had a common interest with Members of Parliament in creating and maintaining an effective political machine) and one can see that no government would be much interested in ringing the changes until it became crystal-clear that the existing local government structure simply could not cope with the scale of problems with which it was faced.

By the mid-sixties the decision could be postponed only for the length of time a Royal Commission would sit. It was at last recognised that many local authorities quite simply lacked the resources, financial and manpower, to provide the required level and quality of service. Planning decisions were being made in isolation and there was a marked lack of any form of integrated approach to common problems by neighbouring authorities, except in certain fields such as further education where a regional machinery had been created to force local authorities to make collective decisions. With few exceptions, there was little attempt, even within authorities, to integrate the various services to see how to promote schemes that were coordinated between the different areas of the Authority's activities. It is not true, of course, to say that there was *no* coordination: if a new housing estate was to be developed, drains would be laid, a school would be planned and built, bus services would be provided, perhaps even a branch library or a health clinic would also be erected. But there was little or no concept of a total plan for the development of the area covered by the Authority, or a programme to show which parts of the plan would be implemented at a given time so that the full range of activities could be judged as a whole, and priorities worked out in the interests of the whole community. The 1960s in Britain was the decade of rationalisation – the Ministry of Technology was formed to help industry to reorganise itself to face the modern world; the Department of Economic Affairs to help us plan the country's future; health and social security were brought together. Management consultants abounded, preaching new styles of management, new tools of management. Efficiency was the catchword. It was not a world into which local government with its cosy and fusty image could be readily fitted. Change had become inevitable.

There are two fundamental dilemmas facing local government. The first is how to have democratic control, with elected members able to decide between all major options for the development of the area controlled by the Authority, and yet have efficient management by the paid professionals. The other is how to divide the country up into administrative units which will reflect socio-geographical units, be big enough to allow for sensible planning and development, be small enough for the personal services provided by local authorities not to be remote, and yet to have a single system throughout the country. If local government was to be meaningfully reformed these two problems had to be faced up to and, whilst it is recognised that it is not possible to reconcile all the conflicting aims, the best compromise had to be sought. Various committees and Royal Commissions were appointed by the Government of the day to investigate these areas and to make recommendations.[1]

Although the debate on the structure of local government is now resolved, in that authorities in England, Wales and Scotland have been reorganised, it is necessary, if we are to appreciate fully the continuing controversy about the ability of local authorities to achieve their objectives and to 'act responsibly', to rehearse the arguments for the different approaches put forward. The major alternatives were presented by the Redcliffe-Maud Commission majority report, by its one dissenting member, Mr Derek Senior, and by the Conservative Government whose proposals were in the event enacted.

The Redcliffe-Maud report

The Redcliffe-Maud Commission found four major faults with local government as it was organised at the time of their investigations and deliberations. Although Mr Senior was unable to agree with his colleagues' proposals for the future, he agreed with their analysis of the existing system. The faults were:

(i)   Local government areas do not fit the pattern of life and work in modern England. The gap will widen as social, economic and technological changes quicken.

(ii)   The fragmentation of England into seventy-nine county boroughs and forty-five counties, exercising independent jurisdictions and dividing town from country, has made the proper planning of development and transportation impossible. The result has often been an atmosphere of hostility between county boroughs and counties and this has made it harder to decide difficult questions on their merits.

(iii)   The division within each county between county council and a number of county district councils, together with the position of county boroughs as islands in the counties, means that services which should be in the hands of one authority are fragmented among several. The difficulties of meeting comprehensively the needs of families and individuals is thus greatly increased.

(iv)   Many local authorities are too small, in size and revenue, and in consequence too short of highly qualified manpower and technical equipment to do their work as well as it could and should be done.[2]

The Commission also pointed out defects in the relationships between local government and the national government, and local government and the public. Local government, in fact, was regarded by many people as irrelevant because it was unable to resolve their problems, and by central government as not being able to run local affairs and as being unable to discuss issues with central government with any degree of unanimity because of the vastly different types of authority.

The first three faults were not unfortunate accidents of the passage of time: they were built into the structure from its very creation. They resulted from a determination by the groups dominating Parliament at the end of the nineteenth century to prevent urban areas resolving their problems at the expense of rural areas. There is one important similarity between this and the new structure now prevailing as will be seen when we describe the present system. The Redcliffe-Maud research team, in their discussion of the changing relationship of town and country, quote from a book on local government and taxation, published in 1885: 'No readjustment of boundaries can be satisfactory which ignores the manifold differences between urban and rural districts. Whatever areas be adopted they must not be so designed as to force straggling villages into a . . . union with populous towns.'[3]

This whole concept was roundly rejected by the Redcliffe-Maud Commission. Their researchers produced various maps which demonstrated the mobility of people, and the Commission pointed out that people from the countryside go into towns for shops, entertainment, higher education and many professional services; people who work in towns frequently live in the countryside; and that people who live in towns use the countryside for recreation. Thus the *whole* needs of people could only be met by recognising the interrelationship of town and country.

Few people, if any, other than those who served them as members or officers, would disagree with the contention that many authorities were too small and thus lacked adequate resources. It is difficult to believe that the 1,490 residents of Tintwistle Rural District were provided with a comprehensive housing service giving guidance on house purchase, mortgages, facilitating exchanges and the like, as well as owning and renting houses. It is equally difficult to believe that the smallest education authorities were able to provide the support services of advisers, teachers' centres, reprographic units, and so on, which are a feature of the best authorities. So, yes, some authorities were too small. But what should the optimum size be? To some extent that depended on the sort of authority to be created and this was the point where views started to diverge.

Since the last local government reorganisation, debate had raged about whether it was preferable to have unitary authorities or to have two levels of authority. In other words, whether it was more appropriate to have one authority to be responsible for all services within a given geographical area or whether it was better to divide the responsibilities between two levels. The Association of Municipal Corporations who represented the interests of the urban areas favoured unitary authorities; the County Councils Association favoured two-tier authorities. They had remained in these entrenched positions from their earliest days in Victorian times, right through to the 1960s. Indeed many people argue that it was their intransigence and refusal to come to any agreement, that prevented the otherwise long-awaited local government reform. Governments said that they wanted the local authority associations to agree amongst themselves before national government imposed changes. Indeed, Richard Crossman said as much when he was first made minister. He was later to realise what was there for all to see: that if government awaited that agreement, local government might never be reformed. He therefore established the Redcliffe-Maud Commission.

The majority of the Commission were in no doubt: the unitary authority, whilst posing difficulties – and indeed not proving possible in the major conurbations – was much to be preferred to two-tier authorities. They quote the Seebohm Report on the Social Services: 'The counties through their welfare departments are responsible for homeless families but have no direct access to local authority housing . . . Any successful policy for the homeless depends entirely upon good cooperation between a county and perhaps as many as twenty or thirty district housing authorities in its area. With goodwill and effort it can be achieved but the hazards are considerable and not always overcome.'[4]

Only by having unitary authorities can planning functions be exercised properly: how can an authority plan and develop its area if it has no responsibility for housing? But the Commission claimed that it was not only physical manifestations that showed up the deficiencies of two-tier local government, it showed up in the type of thinking. 'No single authority is responsible for considering the community as a whole. So county and district councils are, inevitably, providers of services rather than proper units of local government.'[5]

Mr Derek Senior did not agree with his colleagues that a pattern of all-purpose authorities would enable essential functions to be discharged effectively nor that it would create a structure in which local democracy could be sustained. In some areas he felt unitary authorities would be too small for planning and development purposes; in others too big for the personal services (i.e. housing, education, social services and the like) to be able to respond to local need. For Mr Senior the best approach was to analyse functional and democratic needs in relation to the patterns of settlement, activity and community structure in which a motor age society organises itself. Thus, for planning, transportation and development purposes one would look at major centres and define the hinterlands they serve, whilst for the personal services one would define areas in terms of accessibility and population size. He thus recommended that the country be divided into thirty-five directly elected regional authorities and one hundred and forty-eight district councils, again directly elected. In four areas, based on Shrewsbury, Peterborough, Cambridge and Lincoln, the same authority would exercise regional and district responsibilities. The regional authorities would be responsible for planning, transportation, development, capital investment programming and education. District councils would be responsible for such services as health, personal social services, housing management and consumer protection.

Mr Senior's proposals bore strong similarities to those of the Royal Commission on Local Government in Scotland, which met under the chairmanship of Lord Wheatley. The Wheatley Commission rejected 'all-purpose' authorities because, whilst they had the advantages of being easy to understand and operate, they did not fit the geographical and social facts of Scotland. The Commission felt that the authorities would be too big for personal services or too small for large-scale services. Thus, they also proposed a two-tier system comprising regional and district authorities.

The Consultative Document *The Reform of Local Government in Wales*, published by the Conservative Government in 1971, also rejects unitary authorities.

Many important services are most effectively organised on a large scale. This permits the recruitment of specialised staff and makes for economy in operation. Further, people expect a general uniformity in the standard of service provided by local authorities wherever they live. These considerations point to having strong authorities, serving sizeable populations and covering substantial areas of the country. It is necessary to take into account also geographical considerations, historical associations and the strength of community feeling. Some services, however, can be dealt with quite adequately on a more local scale; and the Government consider that there is every justification for district councils with clear cut executive responsibilities to run these services. They are firmly opposed to monolithic authorities, which moreover, would deny opportunities of local public service to all save a few.[6]

This philosophy reflected Conservative opinion on the reform of local government in England and Scotland as well and, indeed, the Conservative party included a commitment to reform local government on a two-tier basis in its manifesto for the 1970 general election.

The majority of the Redcliffe-Maud Commission felt that it was important to define what should be the normal maximum and minimum populations of authorities. They felt that the minimum population capable of supporting the range of resources necessary was 250,000; and that the maximum beyond which the personal services would become too remote was about a million. Mr Senior felt that to define size of authority in this way was artificial. He felt that the socio-geographic definition of areas which he proposed would determine the best size for any given area. To him concepts such as maximum and minimum sizes were irrelevant. To the majority of the Commission his concept of socio-geographic regions placed too great an emphasis on a factor which they felt should merely be taken into account with other factors when actually defining the boundaries of each authority's area.

The new structure
The Conservative Government did not accept Mr Senior's concept of city-regions, but neither did they accept the majority report's recommendations of unitary authorities within established ranges of population. They divided the country into two-tier authorities, the populations of many of which fell significantly outside Redcliffe-Maud's recommendations. The Redcliffe-Maud Commission had accepted that there were some major concentrations of population where their concept of unitary authorities was not practical. These were the areas around Birmingham, Manchester and Liverpool. For these metropolitan areas, the Commission accepted that there needed to be two levels of authority as for some purposes they were indivisible whilst for others they were too vast and unwieldy. The concept of metropolitan county areas was one which the Government took up and developed in its own way. England is now divided into metropolitan counties and non-metropolitan counties, each being sub-divided into districts. Scotland is divided into regions and sub-divided into districts but also has three more-or-less all-purpose authorities for the Orkney and Shetland Islands and the Western Isles. Table 1.2. and Figures 1.1. and 1.2. summarise the position.

It has already been said that the size of many of the new authorities did not fall within the parameters established by Redcliffe-Maud (though it must be said that these were established by listening to various specialised viewpoints and then 'feeling' that the stated extremes were right, rather than on any more objective basis). All of the metropolitan counties exceed one million population (the biggest, West Midlands, being 2,790,000). Four non-metropolitan counties are over a million (Kent with 1,396,000 being the biggest). Whilst none of the non-metropolitan counties falls below Redcliffe-Maud's minimum of 250,000, no fewer than thirteen of the metropolitan districts, which have responsibility for education and social services, fall below that figure, and the smallest, Bury, has only 180,000. There are many who feel that these authorities will rapidly become the 'new poor' who will lack resources and be unable to attract the best manpower available. And yet, in its White Paper, the Government had said 'The units appropriate to the provision (of education and social services)

Table 1.2. *The new local government structure*

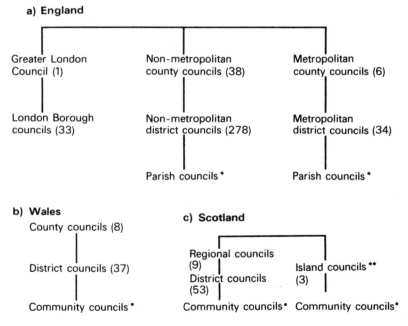

*Parish and community councils exist in some, but not all, districts.
**Police and fire services are provided in conjunction with the mainland authorities, as are the more specialised aspects of education and social services.

Fig. 1.1. *Counties in England and Wales*

(*County Councils Gazette*, 1972)

should have populations broadly within the range 250,000 to one million. These limits should not be inflexible but it should be only in special circumstances that these services are provided by units below this size'.

The areas which were to be allowed to administer these services and yet be below the 250,000 mark, are for the most part those industrial towns in the Midlands and the North of England which grew up in the wake of the Industrial Revolution and now have higher than the normal number of problems, both social and environmental, and poor rateable values. Critics of the Government's proposals found it difficult to work out what the special circumstances were which places such as Barnsley, Bury, Gateshead, St Helens, Oldham and the like shared, and which would enable them to provide the full range of services despite their smallness.

The Government accepted that there needed to be a bringing together of town and country – to abolish what Redcliffe-Maud had called a 'pock-marked' administrative pattern – and the new non-metropolitan counties therefore include the towns and cities that lie within their boundaries. For those functions exercised at county level, the major ones being planning, most of transportation, education and social services, the opportunity now exists to view town and country as an entity.

However, the same cannot be said of the metropolitan counties. We said earlier that the Government had taken the Redcliffe-Maud proposal to create metropolitan counties and had adapted that proposal to its own end. For a start it increased the number from three to six, adding South Yorkshire, West Yorkshire and Tyne-and-Wear to the original proposal of South-East Lancashire (now called Greater Manchester), Merseyside and the West Midlands. Its purpose in doing that seems to have been to separate off these six massive urban areas and to contain them within very tight bounds. An example of this could be the West Midlands. The Redcliffe-Maud recommendation was to create a metropolitan county for the great industrial area surrounding Birmingham and the 'breathing space' to its west and south-west. The Conservative Government's proposal was to create a fairly tight urban community. If we put the proposals alongside each other the point becomes clearer. (See Table 1.3.)

Table 1.3.

Redcliffe-Maud proposal	Actual West Midland Metropolitan County
1 County boroughs Birmingham, Dudley, Solihull, Walsall, Warley, West Bromwich, Wolverhampton	Same (Warley and West Bromwich combined as Sandwell) plus Coventry
2 Non-county boroughs Lichfield, Stafford, Tamworth, Bewdley, Kidderminster	None
3 Urban districts Two in Staffordshire Three in Worcestershire	None
4 Rural districts Four in Staffordshire Two in Worcestershire Parts of three in Warwickshire	Part of one in Warwickshire (Meriden)

That it was deliberate policy to confine the metropolitan areas is not in doubt. Such initial proposals as the Government put up to allow Greater Manchester and, to a lesser extent, Merseyside Metropolitan Counties to take in part of Cheshire, were for the most part removed from the Local Government Bill as it passed through its various stages. The wishes of Cheshire County Council and the various district councils affected were almost entirely accepted despite the protests of the urban areas.

The division of opinion was clear: on the one hand were those who believed that the urban giants had to be contained if we were to prevent England becoming an urban sprawl between London and South Lancashire and South Yorkshire: on the other were those who believed that these urban giants, products of the Industrial Revolution and Victorian development, could only resolve their development problems in a manner that would enable their citizens to lead full lives if they were allowed to expand beyond the close confines of their existing boundaries. It was a division that had a familiar ring about it and, as in 1888, the 'county' argument won.

In the allocation of functions between the two levels of authority, the Government paid regard to the size of the authority rather than the relationship of one service to another. It was a problem which the Redcliffe-Maud Commission had pointed out: it was not really possible over the country as a whole to get both the right relationship *and* the right size. They had chosen to give over-riding importance to relationship – hence their decision to recommend unitary authorities and, in the opinion of Derek Senior anyway, to give only secondary importance to the size and geography of the areas. The Government voted to give services to the areas which were most appropriate in terms of size.

Table 1.4. *Allocation of major functions between different tiers of authority in metropolitan, non-metropolitan and Welsh counties after local government reorganisation, 1974.*

Activity	Metropolitan counties	Non-metropolitan counties	Wales
Transport coordination Major planning Highways Traffic Consumer protection	County	County	County
Refuse collection Local planning Cemeteries & crematoria Building regulations Housing Environmental health	District	District	District
Land acquisition Museums & art galleries Parks and open spaces Playing fields and swimming baths	Shared between county and district		
Education	District	County	County
Social services	District	County	County
Transport undertakings	County	District	District
Consumer protection	County	County	District
Refuse disposal	County	County	District

It will be seen in Table 1.4. that whilst in many cases this led to the decision to allocate a particular service to the same level in metropolitan, non-metropolitan and Welsh counties alike, for other services the 'appropriate level' was determined by reference to the size of the authority. Thus, housing has been deemed to be the responsibility of district councils whatever the size of the district. In contrast, the metropolitan counties are thought to be too big in terms of population to handle social services and education and the non-metropolitan districts and Welsh districts are thought to be, on the whole, too small. Thus, responsibility has been given to the county councils in the non-metropolitan counties in England and Wales, but to the district councils in the metropolitan county areas. It is not easy to understand why Welsh county councils were thought to be inappropriate for handling consumer protection and refuse disposal, whereas both are the responsibility of the county councils in England, whether these counties are metropolitan or non-metropolitan.

Probably the most controversial of the decisions on the allocation of duties was that to give non-metropolitan district councils responsibility for housing and the county councils responsibility for social services (and, though not so emphatically argued, education). The case put forward by critics of the decision was that housing policy frequently had important consequences for social services departments and should therefore be decided by the same council that bore responsibility for social services. This brings us to the corporate management philosophy of reviewing all policies with the consequences upon other services being borne in mind and not merely the effect on the department concerned. A housing policy, for example, which had the effect of creating problem ghettos in towns and cities needs to be reviewed not merely in terms of its innate 'fairness' or otherwise, but also in terms of what resources social services and education departments would have to allocate to such ghettos. It is of interest that one of the first items identified for consideration by ministers in the 1974 Labour government within the *Joint Framework for Social Policy* was 'The relationship between housing policy and other social services'.

Scotland
In Scotland, a somewhat more flexible approach has been adopted

Fig. 1.2. *Local Government (Scotland) Act 1973*
Regions and districts

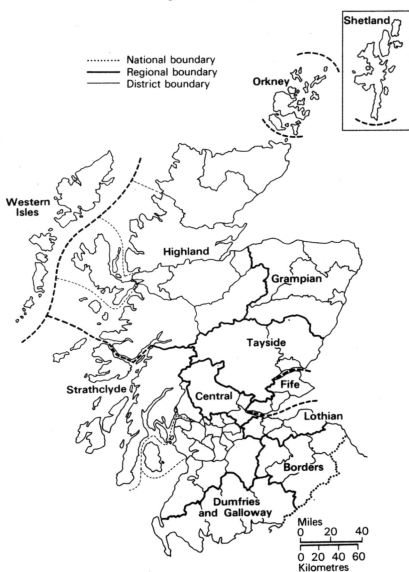

in assigning functions between Regions and Districts. Broadly speaking, they are the same as the distribution between non-metropolitan counties and districts. Regional authorities are responsible for major planning, industrial development, transportation, water supply and sewerage. They also provide education, social services, police and fire services, and are responsible for coastal protection and consumer protection. The districts are almost exactly the same as their English and Welsh counterparts except that in the Highlands, Dumfries and Galloway, and Border regions, the regional rather than district authorities have responsibility for local plans.

London

The one part of the country not described in detail yet is Greater London. Here reorganisation took place somewhat earlier – in 1965. Once again the structure is a two-tier one: the equivalent of the county councils is the Greater London Council (GLC) and of the districts, the thirty-two London boroughs and the City of London. With a few important exceptions, the powers of each level are the same as in metropolitan areas.

The major differences are
1   Education in Inner London (the old London County Council area) is the responsibility of a body called the Inner London Education Authority which is a special independent committee of the GLC. The outer boroughs however, like their metropolitan equivalents, are the education authorities.
2   Whilst housing is principally the responsibility of the boroughs, the GLC has a considerable role to play. In the first instance, it inherited a substantial housing stock from the old LCC and it also has a strategic role in slum clearance and 'overspill'.
3   The boroughs are responsible for consumer protection.

Just as the Redcliffe-Maud boundary proposals were significantly amended so that metropolitan county boundaries were much tighter, so London had been more tightly defined than recommended. The Herbert Commission which had made recommendations for a council with strategic powers saw its definition of the area to be governed by that strategic authority amended by the removal of nine councils, all more rural than any left in. Ten years after its creation a campaign is building up to transfer many of the powers of the GLC to the boroughs. In particular, it is argued that the Inner London Education Authority should be abolished and its power transferred to the separate inner London boroughs. The opponents of this scheme argue that the ILEA is able to redistribute assets from wealthier boroughs such as Kensington and Chelsea to poorer ones such as Tower Hamlets. Proponents of the scheme argue that redistribution should be accomplished through government grants. The other prime candidate for transfer is the GLC role in housing. Critics feel that housing management would be more efficient and more sensitive if it was a responsibility of the boroughs and, whilst accepting the need for a 'London strategy' on housing supply and replacement, they argue that it would be better achieved by a joint committee of the boroughs. It must be accepted that the achievements of the GLC in providing a counterweight to the inequalities in housing in rich and poor boroughs have not been adequate.

Critics of the GLC role in education and housing argue the more basic point that its involvement in small decisions hinder it in its proper role of strategic authority. Whether any national government would allow it the sort of powers it would need to be fully effective, is doubtful indeed. At the moment, governments determine the allocation of capital grants and determine employment and industrial policy in the light of their overall economic policy. It is difficult to believe that they will be prepared to lose control in these policy areas on the vast scale that devolution of power to the GLC would involve. Given that a prime cause of the distress felt by many of the Conservatives (and Labour ministers) is that the Labour-controlled GLC increased its rates precept by 80 per cent in 1975, it is not likely that *these* critics will seek to enhance the powers of the GLC, even if the enhancement is counterbalanced by it being shorn of its powers in other areas.

Ad hoc authorities

We have argued earlier that powers allocated to, or taken away from, local government are gained or lost, not because of any philosophy of the role of local government within a democratic society, but rather because of the national government's wish to re-organise a particular service. As a result of the 1974 reorganisation, the powers exercised by local authorities in water supply and sewage disposal were transferred to newly created Regional Water

Authorities, and local authority powers in providing various health services were also transferred to newly-created Area Health Boards. The local authorities saw this as a blow and they were deeply resentful of what they regarded as attempts by national government to 'cut them down to size'. The Policy Committee of the Association of Metropolitan Authorities wrote in a memorandum to the Department of Health and Social Security in the summer of 1974:

> During the passage of the National Health Service Reorganisation Act through Parliament, the previous Secretary of State, Sir Keith Joseph, admitted that ideally the health services should be unified within local government. The decision not to integrate the NHS with local government, at the same time as the transfer of water and sewage to regional bodies, was seen by the local Authority Associations as a major set-back and misfortune for democratic local government at a time when the paramount need was to provide a strong and comprehensive new structure and to reverse the trend of local government services to the centre or to *ad hoc* bodies.[7]

The basic criticism of these bodies is that they are not directly answerable to the electorate for their actions. At best, they have democratically elected councillors nominated to them; at worst, they have members nominated by the Secretary of State for the Environment (whose powers of patronage are vast!) or by groups who are answerable to no one except themselves. The Government saw fit to change control by democratic means to control by special interest groups. There was no dispute about the need to unify the health service, only about how to make the unified service more answerable for its actions. Claims for improved efficiency are made but it is too early to say whether they will be realised. Following the creaction of *ad hoc* bodies to control police and fire services, listening to the rising cry for transfer of significant services such as education to the national government, and seeing the transfer of health, sewage and water to regional bodies (though not in Scotland), local authorities are perhaps right to be fearful for the future.

authorities to show whether they can manage corporately, whether they can accommodate changes and demands for new services in a more restricted financial climate. If the local authorities are able to show that they can respond sensitively to the wishes of their electorate, not merely by expanding as in the past, but by a redefinition of responsibilities and priorities, their future must surely be secure.

2 Regionalism and nationalism

Regionalism and nationalism are expressions that have become part of the United Kingdom's political vocabulary in the last ten to fifteen years. Most politicians have felt constrained to make some, more or less grudging, commitment to the principles of regionalism and nationalism. Yet, it is clear that both politicians and public are confused by the various interpretations of what constitutes regionalism or nationalism: the expressions mean different things to different people. Agreement that there is a distinctive sense of nationhood in Scotland, for instance, does not imply agreement on the best range of political institutions to cater for that sense of nationhood. One of the purposes of this chapter, therefore, is to analyse the various different political theories and institutions that tend to be indiscriminately referred to as regionalism and nationalism in the United Kingdom.

Before turning to this analysis, it is worth emphasising that the increased preoccupation with regionalism and nationalism shown by the United Kingdom Government and Parliament in recent years, has had very little to do with the academic and technical arguments. Westminster and Whitehall have reacted to more directly political factors, in particular the electoral fortunes of the Nationalist parties. The Royal Commission on the Constitution – which, in spite of its title, concerned itself almost entirely with the issues of regionalism and nationalism – was set up in April 1969. It was seen by many as a response to the by-election victories of the Welsh Nationalists at Carmarthen in 1966, and the Scottish Nationalists at Hamilton in 1967. These two parties also had considerable success in local government elections: for instance in May 1968, the Scottish Nationalist Party polled nearly 180,000 votes in Edinburgh, Aberdeen, Dundee and Glasgow, while the

Labour Party polled just under 130,000. The Royal Commission was considered by many to be a device selected by the Labour Government in order to show that the Government was in fact reacting to the wishes of the people, as expressed in the elections, but also in order to delay any positive action in the hope that the Nationalist electoral challenge would fade away. The Royal Commission finally reported in 1973, and was at first almost totally ignored, for by this time the Nationalist challenge seemed to have faded: only one Nationalist candidate had been elected in the 1970 General Election. However, the results of the 1974 General Elections caused the report to be rather hastily resurrected from whatever dusty Whitehall pigeon-hole to which it had been consigned. Those elections saw a major increase in the number of Welsh and Scottish Nationalist M.P.s, as well as the emergence of the United Ulster Unionists as a group no longer formally associated with the Conservative Party. Between the two 1974 elections, these groups effectively held the balance of power in the House of Commons. The Government's response was immediate: the appointment of a special adviser on constitutional matters, and the publication of a White Paper on Devolution. Regardless of the basic arguments, therefore, positive action only occurred when the Government felt that its own political power base, in terms of Parliamentary seats in Scotland and Wales, was being threatened.

Principles

The issues that are at stake when we consider the need for 'regional' or 'national' governments within the United Kingdom are many, and basic to the whole analysis of government. The issues are of precisely the same type as fall to be considered when examining the case for *local* government. Just as we might ask if there is a need for local government, rather than having all powers exercised by a central government, so we can ask if there is a need for intermediate government. (Intermediate government will be used to refer to government at the 'regional' or 'national' level, i.e. the level between local government and the United Kingdom government.) If a system of government is to operate effectively, it requires legitimacy: the acceptance of the system by the people, and their support for it. Legitimacy itself is partly a function of the sense of identification felt by the individual citizen with the area of

government. Thus Palestinian Arabs in Israel do not accept the
legitimacy of the Israeli Government, as they feel no sense of
identification, no sense of community, with the state of Israel. On
the other hand, virtually all inhabitants of Scotland, England and
Wales consider themselves British, and identify with the Government of the United Kingdom. In practice, people identify with a
number of different communities: an individual may see himself as
British, as a Londoner, and as living in Hampstead Village. Thus, he
may identify with the UK Government, with the Greater London
Council, but not necessarily with Camden Borough Council which
contains areas other than Hampstead Village, areas with which he
feels no particular affinity apart from the fact that they are also in
London. William Hampton, in his book *Democracy and Community*, shows clearly that most people define their home area in terms of
their village or the few streets in their immediate neighbourhood.
Many local authorities are larger than this and thus have no real
meaning in terms of local community identification. As far as
intermediate government and a public sense of identity are
concerned, however, feelings of regional identification are fairly
strong throughout the country. 'Although they are particularly
strong in Wales and Scotland, they are almost as marked in the
South West and Yorkshire.'[1] Intermediate government may therefore be able to claim legitimacy through public identification.

Active public support for a system of government also demands
that the system be democratic, that the governors are publicly
accountable, that they are subject to public control and influence,
that the public can participate in a real sense in decision-making,
that the public are free to express their opinions, and that all
members of the public have equal rights within the political system.
Such institutions of intermediate government as exist at present –
the regional water authorities, for example – can hardly be said to be
subject to any genuine public control, and the mechanisms for
public accountability are complex and attenuated. As far as public
participation is concerned, a number of surveys, particularly those
undertaken for the Maud Committee on Management and for the
Royal Commission on the Constitution, have shown that a larger
proportion of the electorate feel they could contribute to
decision-making, as councillors for instance, than actually do so
contribute. Twenty-six per cent of those questioned in the Royal

Commission's Attitude Survey thought they could do as good a job as the average councillor, and sixty-seven per cent thought that there should be more opportunity for ordinary people to become councillors. In addition, surveys have also shown that most people would welcome any steps to move decision-making to a more regional or local level, in the belief that this would allow more popular participation and control. In the Attitude Survey seventy-six per cent considered that, if the regions had more say in running their own affairs, then the ordinary man would have more say in deciding what is done. Other evidence shows that the British public have a strong desire to participate in any institution that affects them. At least half the population belong to at least one voluntary organisation, and ten per cent or more are office-holders in such organisations; over seventy per cent of those employed by large organisations consider that they should have more say in the way the job is done; and seventy per cent of people consider that they do not have enough say in the way the Government runs the country and the way local authorities handle things. This adds up to a strong desire for participation in government, a desire that is not being satisfied at present. The other main element of democracy that needs to be considered is equality, that each individual has equal rights and an equal share in government. Some schemes for intermediate government may offend against this principle. For instance, the existence of a Scottish Assembly having control over certain matters while Scotland continued to send M.P.s to the Westminster Parliament could be said to give more rights to the citizen in Scotland than to his counterpart in England.

Schemes for intermediate government must also show awareness of one of the major features of the British system of government: the concept of Parliamentary sovereignty. Our present system means that Parliament can legislate on any matter, and that Ministers are responsible to Parliament for the implementation of legislation. This has implications for intermediate government that will be considered below. This unitary nature of the constitution tends to lead to uniformity: similar cases are expected to be treated similarly. If a Member of Parliament asks why a particular matter has been treated differently in Oxfordshire than in Lancashire, he will not normally expect, or be satisfied by, the reply that Oxfordshire is not Lancashire. On the other hand, the United

Kingdom is a collection of diverse cultures and there may be no real
reason why such diversity should not be recognised in decision-
making. The difficulty, as ever, is in balancing the pressure for
universal minimum standards against the desire for local control.
Although seventy-three per cent of those questioned in Scotland by
the Royal Commission's Attitude Survey agreed with the idea of a
Scottish Assembly, only one-sixth of them were still prepared to
support the idea if it resulted in a reduction in their standards of
living. Such evidence means that the case for intermediate
government must be based on the argument that it would lead to
better government, in terms of legitimacy, of public control, of
participation, of equality, and of efficiency.

Methods

Before examining the existing and proposed institutions of intermediate government in the United Kingdom in the light of the
above analysis, it is necessary to consider the possible methods of
sharing power within a state. The governmental process, put very
simply, consists of the formulation of policy, the enactment of
legislation based on that policy, the determination of how that
legislation shall be implemented or executed, and the routine
administration of the implementation. Some or all, of these four
stages may become the responsibility of intermediate government.
Parliament could transfer responsibility in one of three ways:

Separatism By transferring complete sovereignty in all matters,
thereby effectively creating a separate independent state. This
suggestion has been made in relation to Scotland, Wales, and
Northern Ireland (but not, of course, the English regions) on the
grounds that they are separate and distinct nations that were
incorporated into the United Kingdom more or less unwillingly.

The creation of separate, independent states in this way would
not be unprecedented, for it is precisely what was done with the
creation of the Irish Free State, now the Republic of Ireland. The
experience of Eire is often overlooked when the transfer of powers
from the Westminster Parliament is being considered. Although
Eire has inevitably had to adjust many of its policies, especially
economic policies, to fit in with United Kingdom policies (the Irish
money market is tied to London and the two currencies are

interchangeable), it has been able to select its own policies in the field of social and cultural legislation. Scotland, Wales and Northern Ireland are even more tied than Eire to the English economy since virtually all their trade is with England; public expenditure per head is higher than in England although tax revenue per head is lower. Thus, leaving aside the unknown economic effects of North Sea Oil, separate states of Scotland, Wales and Northern Ireland would have to follow English economic policies or choose the independence of a stagnating economy and a declining standard of living. Social policies, too, require finance for their implementation, and this will be less readily available. These are economic rather than political arguments, but political views are formed to a very considerable extent on the basis of a consideration of material interests and we have already seen that only twelve per cent of Scots favour devolution if they would be worse off as a result.

Federalism Rather than transferring complete sovereignty in all matters, Parliament could transfer sovereignty in certain matters only, retaining others such as defence and foreign affairs. In a federal system, the central government is sovereign in some matters while the provincial governments are sovereign in others: neither is subordinate to the other. Examples of countries with such a system include the United States of America, Canada, Australia and West Germany.

Federal systems require a written constitution, setting out the rights of each level of government, a special procedure for constitutional amendments, such as a referendum or a specially large majority in the legislatures at each level, and a constitutional court, which settles any dispute between the levels of government as to their respective powers. There will, in addition, be special arrangements for the distribution of tax revenues, and the Upper House of the central legislature may be constituted in a way that gives particular weight to the provincial interests. Most of these characteristics are unknown in our present system of government, and are certainly not compatible with the concept of the sovereignty of Parliament. Recent experience in countries with federal constitutions has shown that the increased responsibilities of governments have led in some instances to the gradual breakdown of the federal system. 'Provincial governments can no longer keep *de facto* control over all the matters which are constitutionally their sole responsibility. Their sovereignty is being eroded because their electorates are demanding more than can be provided without federal help.'[2] The enforced integration of education in all states of the USA is an example. Schemes for cooperation between provincial and federal governments are introduced which observe the letter rather than the spirit of the constitution, in theory leaving the powers of the provinces intact but in practice putting the federal government in a controlling position. One of the major reasons for this is the fact that provincial governments tend to need more money than is directly available to them. 'One of the chief obstacles to the proper working of federalism is the impracticability of arranging a division of finance between the federal and provincial governments which will for any length of time satisfactorily match their respective functions under the constitution.'[3] In spite of this, there are successful federal systems. However, it may be that the federalists' objectives can be achieved without the inflexibilities of a federal constitution by the third method of sharing power within a state.

Devolution Parliament could retain sovereignty in all matters, while delegating to intermediate governments the exercise of certain selected powers. Such a scheme would acknowledge the unitary nature of the United Kingdom system of government and the supremacy of Parliament, while still leaving certain decisions to be taken at a more local level. The extent of the powers to be devolved could vary broadly as follows.

(a) *Legislative devolution* Under a scheme of legislative devolution provincial assemblies would be given the power to determine policy, to make laws, and implement those laws on a selected range of subjects. Parliament would still have the power to legislate on all matters and a power of veto over provincial legislation, but these powers would rarely need to be exercised. If these reserve powers did not exist, then the system would be a federal system, rather than one of legislative devolution.

(b) *Executive devolution* Under a scheme of executive devolution, Parliament would legislate on all matters but would transfer to provincial assemblies the responsibility for deciding how that legislation would be implemented, its execution, and the formulation of any specific regional policies that did not offend against the national policy framework.

(c) *Administrative devolution* Under a scheme of administrative devolution, Parliament would continue to legislate on all matters but would arrange for the administration of the functions of government to be carried out within a regional setting. This would not involve the creation of provincial assemblies, but would involve a particular type of organisation of central government departments. A scheme of this sort would therefore make no provision for a democratic input at the provincial level.

(d) *Advisory devolution* Under a scheme of this kind, bodies would be established in the provinces to consult with their various local authorities and organisations, to consider appropriate policies, and to advise the central government and Parliament accordingly. In some ways, the task would therefore be similar to the function of a Select Committee in the House of Commons, but constituted on a regional basis.

Intermediate governments
In the light of the principles that might guide any scheme for sharing power within the United Kingdom, and the methods that might be followed, let us now turn to an examination of the forms of intermediate government that already exist in the United Kingdom and of the suggestions that have been made in recent years.

Northern Ireland
The best-known example of intermediate government in the United Kingdom has been the 'Stormont Model' in Northern Ireland, established in 1920, and which lasted until the imposition of direct rule in 1972. This can be regarded as an example of legislative devolution. The Government of Ireland Act 1920 gave the Parliament of Northern Ireland the power to make laws for the peace, order and good government of the province and responsibility for all matters other than those specifically reserved for the Westminster Parliament. The main reserved matters were those relating to the Crown, the making of peace and war, the armed

services, foreign and Commonwealth relations, treason, aliens, overseas trade, merchant shipping, wireless telegraphy, aerial navigation, coinage, trade marks, copyrights, patents, the postal services, customs and excise, income tax, and any tax on profits. Matters not included in this list, therefore, were generally the responsibility of the Northern Ireland Parliament. Legislation enacted by the Parliament at Stormont was carried out by the Government of Northern Ireland, headed by a British-style cabinet. In 1972 the Northern Ireland Government contained nine departments: the Prime Minister's Department and the Ministries of Finance, Home Affairs, Agriculture, Commerce, Education, Development, Health and Social Services, and Community Relations. Northern Ireland's revenues were to be derived from taxes imposed by the Northern Ireland Parliament and what was known as the residuary share of reserved taxation, i.e. Northern Ireland's share of taxes such as income tax, and customs and excise duties after deducting the cost of Northern Ireland's share of reserved services. In addition to the Stormont Parliament, Northern Ireland is represented by twelve members in the UK Parliament.

A study of the operation of the Stormont system between 1920 and 1972 leads to several conclusions. In the first place, the practice of home rule has been rather different from the theory. Northern Ireland has not, on the whole, pursued independent policies, even in those areas where Stormont was responsible for legislation. The pressures for equality of services with the rest of the United Kingdom are very considerable; given that Northern Ireland is poorer than the rest of the United Kingdom and that Stormont has not wished to levy higher taxes than elsewhere in the UK, equality of services has required financial assistance from Westminster. In fact, the financial arrangements in the 1920 Act lasted for a very short time until they were effectively replaced by a system which means that Northern Ireland is 'subsidised' from the UK exchequer, and that expenditure by the Government of Northern Ireland is just as much subject to Treasury control as expenditure by any Whitehall department. Nevertheless – in education, for instance – Northern Ireland has been able to follow policies which diverge from those being followed elsewhere in the UK.

Relationships with other levels of government are also of interest. It is noteworthy that certain services which are operated elsewhere by local authorities have, since 1920, been operated by Stormont or have been transferred to that level. The Local Government Review Body chaired by Sir Patrick Macrory recommended, in 1970, that most of the major local government functions should be transferred to the Northern Ireland Government itself. The economic and efficiency arguments for larger units of local government, noted elsewhere, have found a ready-made solution in Ulster in the form of the Stormont Government. Financial relationships with the United Kingdom Government have already been mentioned; of importance, too, is the electoral relationship. Twelve Ulster M.P.s sit at Westminster, although on a strict population basis it should be seventeen. The number is in fact a compromise embodied in the 1920 Act. Some suggested that, since Ulster had its own Parliament for its domestic affairs, it did not need any representation at all at Westminster. However, all the 'reserved' matters, especially, would be decided at Westminster and would be as important for Ulster as for the rest of the country. Another suggestion was that Ulster should have its rightful proportion of M.P.s, but that they should be able to vote only on 'reserved' matters. The practical difficulties in the context of the complex nature of Parliamentary business ruled this out. The existence of twelve M.P.s free to vote on any matter was the, perhaps unsatisfactory, answer to the problem.

The system of government in Northern Ireland was essentially modelled on that operating in Westminster and Whitehall. However, parliamentary democracy in the United Kingdom has been characterised by the alternation of the political parties in power, with the result that no substantial minority has been permanently in opposition, and the executive has not become identified with one particular party. Northern Ireland, on the other hand, has been a one-party state since the first election there in 1921. The refusal of the minority to continue to accept this situation was probably the crucial factor in the decision of the United Kingdom government to impose direct rule in 1972. The UK Parliament, in passing the 1973 Northern Ireland Constitution Act, was clearly attempting to move Northern Ireland from a one-party government system to a multi-party government system. Particularly important innovations here were the imposition of a proportional representation voting system, and the creation within the new Northern Ireland assembly of multi-party consultative committees whose chairmen would head the relevant government departments. This system lasted for a few months only before collapsing in the face of a strike backed by the 'Loyalists', and the consequent reimposition of direct rule. A study of General Election results will show that one-party dominance may be difficult to avoid in any scheme of election for intermediate governments in the United Kingdom. Since the success of any government ultimately depends upon its acceptance by all the people involved, this is a factor not to be lightly discounted.

The Scottish Office and the Welsh Office
Although the Scottish and Welsh Offices differ from each other in a number of ways, it is convenient to consider them together, for they represent the same type of devolution: administrative devolution. Scotland has enjoyed a greater measure of devolution than Wales, and for a longer period of time. The reasons for this can, no doubt, be found in history, and especially in the fact that Scotland retained political independence until the Act of Union in 1707 while Wales had been dominated by England for centuries prior to that date. Furthermore, while England and Wales share a common legal system, there is a well-defined and independent system of Scottish law.

The office of Secretary of State for Scotland was recreated in 1885 and has been a Cabinet post since 1892. The post of Secretary of State for Wales on the other hand, with Cabinet status, has existed only since 1964. A brief statement of their main responsibilities, indicated by asterisks, is given in Table 2.1., which shows clearly the wider duties of the Secretary of State for Scotland. In both countries other Cabinet ministers also exercise responsibilities. Thus, in Wales only about half of government expenditure falls within the responsibility of the Secretary of State, while in Scotland the figure is nearer two-thirds. The Scottish Office employs 6,500 staff compared with the 1,000 working in the Welsh Office. While the work of the Welsh Office can be carried on in a reasonably integrated unit, the Scottish Office has five distinct departments: Agriculture and Fisheries, Development, Economic Planning, Education, Home and Health. The ministerial team of the Scottish Office is correspondingly larger than the Welsh team, and also includes two Scottish law ministers. In both countries, there are a substantial number of *ad hoc* advisory and executive bodies,

responsible in varying degrees to the Secretary of State.
    How successful have the Scottish and Welsh Offices been? Does

Table 2.1. *The main responsibilities of the
Secretaries of State for Scotland and Wales*

	Scotland	Wales
Agriculture and fisheries	*	* (jointly with Min. of Ag. F F)
Arts and culture	*	* (except Arts Council, local museums and libraries)
Criminal law	*	
Crofting	*	
Crown estates	*	
Education	* (except universities)	* (primary and secondary)
Electricity	*	
Environmental services	*	*
Fire services	*	
Food hygiene and standards	*	
Forestry	*	*
Health	*	*
Highlands development	*	
Housing and building control	*	*
Legal functions	*	
Local government	*	*
Police	*	
Prevention of pollution	*	*
Prisons	*	
Regulatory functions	*	
Roads	*	*
Rural development	*	*
Social work	*	* (except probation and after care)
Sport and recreation	*	*
Transport	* (except road freight and rail)	* (some aspects of road passenger transport)
Tourism	*	*
Town and country planning	*	*
Urban programme	*	*
Youth and community service	*	

their experience suggest that a worthwhile form of intermediate government for the United Kingdom would be one where central government departments are organised on area lines rather than functional lines with Secretaries of State for the various English regions, rather than Secretaries of State for the Environment, for Education, and so on?

In the first place, the Scottish and Welsh Offices have smaller geographic areas and populations to deal with than have the United Kingdom departments. This can mean a greater knowledge of the needs and problems of the area, as well as a better acquaintance with reference to the Scottish Office: 'The Scottish Office tends to follow very closely the administrative patterns laid down in Whitehall. On the other hand, there is evidence that a regional administration dealing with local peculiarities such as the complicated legal tenure of Scottish tenements, can make minor but useful improvements on its own initiative.'[4]

should be able to adapt methods of administration to meet local needs. J.P. Mackintosh, in his *The Devolution of Power*, concludes with reference to the Scottish Office: The Scottish Office tends to follow very closely the administrative patterns laid down in Whitehall. On the other hand, there is evidence that a regional administration dealing with local peculiarities such as the complicated legal tenure of Scottish tenements, can make minor but useful improvements on its own initiative.[4]

The third consideration for judging the success of the Scottish and Welsh Offices is the extent to which they enable local people to feel that they control the way in which they are being governed, and the extent to which they reduce the feeling of discontent with remote, London-based government. Judged in this way, the Scottish and Welsh Offices must be regarded as failures. The Royal Commission's Attitude Survey, for instance, found that in Scotland thirty-four per cent of those questioned thought that there was no such office as the Scottish Office, and a further eighteen per cent thought that such an Office might exist, but had never heard of it themselves. Those who knew of it were largely ignorant of its responsibilities. Similar results were obtained in Wales. Furthermore, the electoral and propaganda successes of the two Nationalist parties indicate that the people of Scotland and Wales do not see the schemes of administrative devolution embodied in the Scottish and

Welsh Offices as giving them effective control over the way in which they are governed. The Secretaries of State are members of the United Kingdom Cabinet responsible to the United Kingdom Parliament, and not responsible to any Scottish or Welsh representative institutions. Administrative devolution has apparently not satisfied the people of Scotland and Wales, principally because it has lacked the political dimension of control by locally elected representatives.

The Scottish and Welsh Grand Committees
At the present time there exist within the House of Commons two Grand Committees, one for Scotland and one for Wales. These could be regarded as institutions operating legislative devolution, but in practice are perhaps more accurately thought of as advisory. The Scottish Grand Committee consists of the seventy-one M.P.s representing Scottish constituencies, and the Welsh Grand Committee of the thirty-six Welsh M.P.s; additional Members may be selected so that the Committee reflects the party balance in the House of Commons as a whole. They meet to take the Second Reading of Bills that deal exclusively with Scotland or Wales – although there are very few in the latter case. They may debate any matter of concern to Scotland or Wales; in addition, the Scottish Grand Committee can debate the estimates for the Scottish Office. Divisions do not normally take place in either Committee. Particular criticisms that have been made of the Grand Committee system are: the time allowed is inadequate; discussions are often on subjects of no real importance or interest; there is no effective procedure for scrutiny of the executive; the feeling of remoteness is strengthened by the fact that the Committees meet in London rather than in Edinburgh or Cardiff. Reforms could be suggested to meet these various criticisms, but one major problem would still remain. In the last resort, the Secretaries of State and the Cabinet are responsible to the United Kingdom Parliament. If the views of the majority in the House of Commons differed from the views of the majority in a Grand Committee, the latter would have to concede to the former. Some writers have suggested that the Grand Committee system should be strengthened and extended so that there would be a Grand Committee for each English Region also. It is worth considering whether such committees could be more than

advisory, and whether the problems outlined above in relation to the Scottish and Welsh Committees would exist in England also.

Local government regions in Scotland

So far, in the discussion of intermediate government in the United Kingdom, it has been assumed that Scotland and Wales constitute regions that should not be further subdivided. While the nationalist case basically rests on the treatment of Scotland and Wales as complete units, some suggestions for regional government have further divided them: for instance, linking South Wales with the Bristol area and North Wales with Merseyside. In fact, the new system of local government in Scotland, which came into operation in 1975, has as its top tier units nine regional councils, with special treatment for the Orkney, Shetland and Western Isles. (See figure 1.2.). Two of the regional councils deserve special mention: the Highland region, as it contains nearly half the land area of Scotland; and the Strathclyde region, as it contains over half the population of Scotland. The success or failure of such councils could be a pointer for other parts of the United Kingdom. At the time of writing, it is too early to judge the effectiveness of the regional councils in Scotland, but it is clear that relationships with the Scottish Office may prove difficult – particularly in the case of Strathclyde, so dominant in terms of resources. J.P. Mackintosh has suggested that there is in fact no room for an all-Scottish institution between the regional councils and central government: that the case for an effective Scottish assembly has been pre-empted by the reorganisation of local government.

What are the implications of this Scottish experience for England? Is there room for intermediate government where Metropolitan County Councils already operate? Would the GLC not unbalance any regional structure in which it was contained? Is it possible to be over-governed?

Regionalism in England

Central Government Departments Central government departments can be organised in a number of different ways: on a client basis, on an area basis, on a functional basis. In the United Kingdom only the Scottish and Welsh Offices have been organised on an area basis, while virtually all other departments have been organised on a functional basis. Most departments have nevertheless found it necessary to establish regional offices. The reasons for this should by now be well known: government is now so complex that decentralisation is necessary for efficiency; knowledge of local conditions or of special cases can prevent bureaucratic inflexibility and lead to greater speed; and the department is enabled to make a contribution to national discussion of regional problems. On the other hand, scope for such decentralisation has been limited by Cabinet and Ministerial responsibility, and by Treasury control. Thus, capital expenditure has to be fitted into a national expenditure programme, administrative decisions must be consistent throughout the country subject only to the discretion of the Minister, and certain decisions are reserved for the Minister by statute.

Although most departments have regional organisations, there is very considerable variation between them as to the precise pattern of regions best suited for their functions. This may be true even within departments. For instance, on its creation in 1971, the Department of the Environment had no fewer than thirteen separate regional organisations. This reflects, among other things, the fact that each different service may require a different size unit of operation for maximum efficiency, and also the fact that in socio-geographic terms, many parts of England do not fit neatly into one region or another. In fact, the regional organisation of most departments reflects administrative necessity rather than a particular desire to cater for regional interests. The extent of delegation to regional offices – normally headed by Controllers, of Assistant Secretary or Principal Executive Officer rank – is greatest where the policy content of the work is least; Controllers are therefore managers, rather than policy makers. Civil servants in the regions, too, owe their first loyalty to their department, not the region. They are unlikely to stand up for the region against departmental headquarters, since that is where they hope their future career lies. The fact of decentralisation suggests the need for intermediate government; its practice indicates a failure genuinely to adapt to local needs and shows a complete lack of any form of direct political control.

Ad hoc authorities There are a number of functions that the

Government has thought best should not be provided directly either by central government departments or by local authorities. Examples of such functions would be those provided by the nationalised industries such as gas and electricity, and also those provided by the Health Service and the Water Authorities. The local authorities were considered to be too small in terms of area and population required for the economic operation of these functions, and lacking in the resources necessary to employ specialist staff and equipment. Central government departments were not considered the appropriate bodies to provide these services, mainly on the grounds that detailed controls would militate against speed and managerial efficiency. So institutions of intermediate government were established. Yet in no single instance do the regional boundaries of any one *ad hoc* authority coincide with those of any other; nor do they coincide with the regional boundaries of any departmental regional structure.

The most recently established *ad hoc* units are concerned with the National Health Service and the Water Service. In England the National Health Service is organised into fourteen Regional Health Authorities, responsible for regional planning of the health service, determining competing priorities, and the design and construction of new buildings. Within each RHA, and financed by them, are Area Health Authorities, whose boundaries are coterminous with the local authorities responsible for social services. The Area Health Authorities are responsible for the planning and operation of the health services, but the day-to-day running is the responsibility of Health Districts, whose boundaries, almost inevitably, do not necessarily correspond with the boundaries of the local government districts. In each Health District there has been established a Community Health Council, which is to represent the views of the consumer: performing a similar function to the Consumer Councils and Committees within the nationalised industries. Half the members of the CHC are appointed by the relevant local government district councils, and half are appointed by the AHA after consultation with voluntary bodies and other organisations. Like the nationalised industries' consumer councils, too, the Community Health Councils have no effective power, and their finance and half their membership is determined by the very body they are supposed to check. The Regional Health Authority is run by a board nominated by the Secretary of State; in turn, the majority of the board of the Area Health Authority are nominated by the RHA, and a minority by the relevant local authority. It should be noted that there are no Regional Health Authorities in Scotland and Wales. There the Area Health Authorities are responsible directly to the Scottish Office and the Welsh Office.

In England, the Water Service is now organised into nine Regional Water Authorities, responsible for water supply, sewage disposal, water conservation, water quality control, navigation and water recreation. The boundaries of the RWAs are largely determined by river catchment and drainage areas. The majority of the members of the RWAs are appointed by the Secretary of State, and the minority by the local authorities within the boundaries of the Regional Water Authority. In Scotland there are no *ad hoc* water authorities, the responsibility belongs with the local government regional councils. In Wales there is one single Welsh National Water Development Authority responsible to the Welsh Office.

The examples of health and water emphasise certain factors common to the various *ad hoc* authorities at regional level. First there is a need for intermediate government. There are functions and problems of government that transcend local government boundaries, but are not suitable for operation by central government departments because these latter are already overworked and the functions and problems require to be dealt with by people with a closer knowledge of the area involved. Secondly, there is an extra-ordinary lack of pattern in the number and boundaries of the various regional organisations. In these circumstances there can be no effective regional planning or calculation of priorities. The situation resembles nineteenth century local government prior to the creation of the multi-purpose local authorities. In a later chapter, emphasis will be placed on corporate and community planning: at present there can be no such planning in the English regions. Thirdly, the *ad hoc* authorities are not subject to adequate political, democratic control. Consumer councils are effectively powerless, members of the various *ad hoc* authorities are nominated and not elected, and Ministerial control is very remote and not accountable to the people in the particular region concerned.

Regional economic planning councils The Regional Economic

Planning Councils and Boards were established in 1964, and have responsibilities that are of an advisory nature. There are eight regions of England for economic planning purposes. The members of the Councils are appointed by the Secretary of State for the Environment, and are normally prominent men in the life of the area. At first there was considerable interest in the work of the Councils, and the Government were able to attract leading figures. In the North-East, for instance, the first Chairman of the REPC was T. Dan Smith, then the outstanding politican in that part of the country. The Councils help in formulating the regional plan and advise on the regional implications of national policies. The Boards consist of the senior regional civil servants of the various government departments, exercising a coordinating role and working with the REPCs.

Whitehall does not have to consult the REPCs before taking decisions that affect the regions; the REPCs cannot adjust the patterns of expenditure by the various departments within their regions; the members of the Councils have no power base of their own independent of central government; the Councils cannot compel local authorities to observe the planning and development strategies contained in the REPCs' plans. This lack of authority and lack of power have meant that the necessary task of regional planning has not been performed.

Redcliffe-Maud, Kilbrandon and the future

In recent years there have been a number of suggestions made for the creation or reform of institutions of intermediate government in the United Kingdom. Some of these have already been mentioned, such as the separatism favoured by the Scottish National Party. Others have been contained in various official publications.

The Royal Commission on Local Government in England, under the Chairmanship of Lord Redcliffe-Maud, was unfortunately not able to give full consideration to the problems of intermediate government, because its terms of reference confined it to considering the structure of local government *in relation to its existing functions*. It was therefore prevented from considering whether any functions at present operated by *ad hoc* authorities or central government departments should be transferred to provincial or regional units. In spite of this restriction, the Commission recommended the creation of eight Provincial Councils, covering areas similar to, but not identical with, those of the existing REPCs. The functions of the Provincial Councils were to be: strategic planning, the settling of priorities in further education, the planning of certain specialist services in education and the social services, planning for the development of tourism, and of cultural and recreational services. The Commission's argument, therefore, was that the local government system needed Provincial Councils, irrespective of whether central government also had a role for them. Members of the Provincial Councils were to be indirectly elected by the local authorities in the area.

One member of the Royal Commission, Derek Senior, disagreed with the proposals of his colleagues and submitted his own Memorandum of Dissent. He too saw a need for Provincial Councils in England, although he suggested that the correct number should be five. He too considered that the principal function of a Provincial Council should be the preparation of a strategic plan, although he thought that this should be much broader and more flexible than the type suggested by his colleagues. He also criticised the proposal of his colleagues that the Provincial Councils should be indirectly elected by the local authorities, on the grounds that what was needed was an independent body thinking in terms of the Province and not just in terms of their own individual local authorities. In his Memorandum of Dissent, and in spite of the terms of reference of the Commission, Senior also briefly considered the implications of a devolution of power by central government. He considered that the transferred powers might well be, 'the location of industrial and office employment, the routing of regional motorways, the selection of sites for new regional cities, the determination of development policies for ports and airports, polytechnics, universities and teaching hospitals, and the settlement of all intra-provincial public investment priorities.'[5] When these were added to strategic and structure planning, he recommended the formation of twelve to fifteen 'large-city-region' or 'sub-provincial' authorities. In his scheme, the responsibilities of his proposed top-tier local authorities would be transferred upwards to this level, thus leaving one single level of local government below the intermediate authorities.

Both Redcliffe-Maud and Senior, therefore, saw the need for

some form of Provincial Councils in England, although they disagreed on their precise nature. However, by the time their report was published, the Royal Commission on the Constitution had been established under the chairmanship of Lord Crowther and, after his death, Lord Kilbrandon. This Commission had wide ranging terms of reference, but specific mention was made of the 'several countries, nations and regions of the United Kingdom' and of 'the administrative and other relationships between the various parts of the United Kingdom'. The Commission interpreted its terms of reference as giving it the task of investigating 'the case for transferring or devolving responsibility for the exercise of government functions from Parliament and the central government to new institutions of government in the various countries and regions of the UK.'[6] Just as the report of the Redcliffe-Maud Royal Commission was not unanimous, so too the Kilbrandon Commission failed to reach complete agreement. Two members, Lord Crowther-Hunt and Professor Peacock, published a Memorandum of Dissent; within the majority, there were also a number of points of disagreement. The Memorandum of Dissent took on added importance with the appointment of Lord Crowther-Hunt as an adviser and then as a Minister in the 1974 Labour Government.

The issues considered by the Commission have been briefly discussed earlier in this chapter. The majority favoured legislative devolution for Scotland and Wales but not for England. The assemblies would be directly elected by the single transferable vote system, and their legislative responsibilities would approximate to those matters currently the executive responsibility of the Secretaries of State for Scotland and Wales. These offices would disappear: executive authority would be exercised by Ministers drawn from and responsible to the assemblies. The over-representation in relation to population of Scotland and Wales in the United Kingdom House of Commons would end. For England, the majority favoured the establishment of regional coordinating and advisory councils, partly indirectly elected by the local authorities and partly nominated. The regions would be those instituted for the Regional Economic Planning Councils. The functions of each council would be to scrutinise, debate and make representations about government policies and activities in relation to the region, including the activities of *ad hoc* bodies, and to coordinate the work of local government, including strategic planning.

Alternatives suggested by individual members of the Kilbrandon Commission were: executive devolution for Scotland, Wales, and the English regions; advisory councils for Scotland and Wales; and a scheme of regional coordinating committees of local authorities in England. The Crowther-Hunt and Peacock Memorandum of Dissent proposed a fully worked-out scheme for the establishment of democratically and directly elected Assemblies and Governments in Scotland, Wales, and five English regions. These Assemblies and Governments would take over nearly all the decentralised activities of central government departments; they would take over the functions of the non-commercial, non-industrial *ad hoc* authorities such as the Regional Health and Regional Water Authorities; they would have some supervisory responsibility for the commercial and industrial *ad hoc* authorities such as the Gas Board and the Electricity Board; they, rather than central government, would have administrative responsibilities for dealing with local government; they would have some financial independence; and, within the framework of United Kingdom legislation, they would formulate policies for their area. This scheme would therefore amount to executive, rather than legislative, devolution.

The Government's response to the Kilbrandon Commission was at first rather uncertain. However, after a series of White Papers, the Scotland and Wales Bill was published, appropriately enough, on St Andrew's Day, 30 November 1976. This was followed in December by a consultative document on devolution and England. The Scotland and Wales Bill clearly faced a difficult journey through Parliament, in view of the reservations and hostility expressed by many Members; nor had the Government ruled out the possibility of submitting the issue to a referendum.

The Bill showed that the Government were proposing a scheme of legislative devolution for Scotland, and a scheme of executive devolution for Wales. Each country was to have an Assembly elected by the existing first-past-the-post system and not by proportional representation. Assembly members would serve for a fixed term of four years; each Westminster constituency would be divided into two or (if its electorate is very large) into three Assembly constituencies. Scotland would thus have an Assembly of about 150 members, and Wales an Assembly of about eighty members.

What are the 'devolved matters' that the two Assemblies will deal with? Broadly speaking, these will be, for both countries:

education (including the arts, libraries and sport, but excluding the universities)

health

social work

water services

local government (excluding a few matters, such as the police service, where local authorities remain responsible to the UK Government)

ancient monuments and historic buildings

the environment (including pollution, new towns, the countryside)

development and industry

agricultural land (including forestry and fisheries)

housing

tourism

transport

fire services

In addition, various law functions will be devolved to the Scottish Assembly. For some of the devolved matters the UK Government will retain certain reserve powers: for instance, in relation to housing rents, rate rebates, industrial investment, and the pay of certain groups of public employees.

The Scottish Assembly will have the power to legislate on devolved matters, the Welsh Assembly will not, although it can concern itself with subordinate legislation. Executive power on devolved matters will rest in Scotland with a 'Cabinet': a group of Assembly members, headed by a Chief Executive. This executive will be advised by subject committees of the Assembly, composed in accordance with the balance of the parties. In Wales, executive power will rest with the Assembly itself. However, the Welsh Assembly will also have a system of advisory subject committees, and the Assembly can decide to give these committees an executive role. The leaders of these committees will meet together in an executive committee. Thus, Scotland, with legislative devolution, will have arrangements resembling those at Westminster; Wales, with executive devolution, will have arrangements resembling those in local government. Scotland and Wales will each have an Ombudsman to investigate complaints against the executive, and a Comptroller and Auditor-General on the Westminster pattern.

One of the most difficult problems in the devolution debate is the question of finance. The Bill proposed that the Assemblies should be able to borrow funds – but only within totals specified by the United Kingdom Parliament. The main source of revenue for the Assemblies would be a block grant voted annually by the United Kingdom Parliament. Thus the Assemblies would have no revenue raising powers of their own. This total dependence upon finance from the central government will cause considerable problems, some of which are discussed in Chapter 3, particularly in relation to the Layfield Report. Furthermore, there will almost inevitably be annual disputes between the Assemblies and the Treasury over the amount of the grant. All disappointments and failures can be blamed on the English-dominated UK Government for providing insufficient finance, a very strong temptation for Assemblies to act irresponsibly.

Probably the most crucial issue in the devolution debate, however, is the possibility of conflict between Cardiff or Edinburgh and Westminster over their respective powers. This problem could be particularly acute in relation to the legislative powers of the Scottish Assembly. The Scotland and Wales Bill made a number of provisions to deal with this question.

(i) If the Government thinks that an Assembly Bill is in conflict with the United Kingdom's international obligations, the Secretary of State issues a certificate to that effect, and the Bill will not receive the Royal Assent.

(ii) If the Government thinks that an Assembly Bill exceeds the Assembly's powers, it can refer the Bill to the Judicial Committee of the Privy Council, whose verdict is final.

(iii) If the Government considers that an Assembly Bill, or subordinate legislation, or executive action, has 'unacceptable' repercussions on non-devolved matters, the Government can set aside, revoke, or issue directives to that effect, subject to the approval of Parliament.

(iv) In addition, once an Assembly Bill has become law, any citizen may challenge it in the courts on the grounds that it is *ultra vires*.

If effective working relationships between the Assemblies and Westminster are to be developed, much will depend on the use of the third of these provisions. If it is used by Governments simply as a means of defeating Assembly proposals to which they are politically opposed, devolution will not exist in any meaningful sense.

Conclusion

Government attitudes to regionalism and nationalism have been largely conditioned by electoral considerations. Discontented voters, especially in Scotland and Wales, have turned from the two major parties to other parties, especially the Nationalists. The Kilbrandon Commission's Attitude Survey, however, shows that people are discontented with the *product* of government: standards of living, levels of employment, housing conditions, etc. They blame the failure of government to satisfy their material aspirations on various causes, such as the remoteness and insensitivity of central government. But, if regional or national elected assemblies were established and material conditions did not improve, discontent would continue but would be explained in another way. Thus the case for devolution should be based not on the grounds that discontent is due to a lack of regional self-government but on the grounds that devolution would lead to better government.

Better government is an elusive concept. What might it involve, in terms of the British system? Three particular points might be picked out. First, there is at the present time an excessive burden on the institutions of central government, leading to inefficiency and delay. Secondly, there is a need to ensure that government policies do take note of the very real differences in the needs of the various parts of the United Kingdom. Thirdly, government should be as democratic as possible: all citizens should have equal rights and privileges, and, perhaps more importantly, institutions of government taking decisions affecting the public should be accountable to representatives of the public. On this analysis, executive devolution along the lines proposed in the Crowther-Hunt and Peacock Memorandum would appear to lead to better government. It recognises the need to reduce the burden on the centre, it allows for different interests in different parts of the UK, it acknowledges that the English should have the same political rights as the Scots and the Welsh, and it highlights the presence of existing regional institutions of government that should be made subject to direct political control. Perhaps the main argument against executive devolution of this type, is that there is no real basis of principle for dividing powers between the UK government and the intermediate government. However, this problem has not stood in the way of sharing powers between Whitehall and local authorities; statutes could also be rewritten so that powers in certain areas could be given to regions rather than Ministers.

Executive devolution is also recommended by some, in preference to legislative devolution, on the grounds that legislative devolution is difficult to achieve in a unitary state. Since Parliament can legislate on any matter, it could choose, if it so wished, to over-rule legislation passed by an intermediate assembly. It is true that Stormont legislation was not vetoed by Westminster. However, whether Parliament could be so restrained if Scotland, Wales, or an English region followed policies diametrically opposed to those of the UK Government, is another matter. Furthermore, of course, the UK Parliament did in the end take powers back from Stormont. It may be, too, that political and financial factors would tend to persuade regional legislatures to comply with United Kingdom standards. The popular pressure for equality of standards in the provision of services, coupled with the financial restrictions involved in demand management by the United Kingdom Government, might well mean that regional assemblies could not show significant differences in legislation. This pressure towards conformity would be further strengthened if reserve powers were retained by, say, the Secretary of State for Scotland. Under the Government's proposals he would be responsible to the House of Commons, not to the Scottish Assembly. How would he use his powers if there were, say, a Labour majority in the Scottish Assembly and a Conservative majority at Westminster?

There is a case for devolution of power – to intermediate government, just as much as to local government. But there can be no simple answer to the problem of finding the right level for each type of decision. Should the wishes of the majority of the people in the UK prevail over the wishes of the majority of the people in a region, in that region? Should a regional majority be able to impose its will on a majority in a county within the region? Whatever answer is finally arrived at, it will not satisfy everybody. The art of the politician, however, is to find those solutions that will gather the most general support or, at worst, acquiescence. In the end, whatever the academic and technical arguments, the decision on devolution will be a political one.

3 Finance

Local government in the national economy

If local government is to be other than a locally based executive arm of the central government, Parliament must not only give local authorities wide discretion within those fields it devolves upon them, it must also give them a considerable degree of financial freedom. As we shall see later, this does not mean that all local finances should be raised locally, but rather that local authorities should have freedom, within broadly determined financial resources, to spend the money as they see fit and that the sources should be sufficiently buoyant to allow the authorities a genuine choice.

Before we examine how the money is raised and spent and how it might be, let us give ourselves a perspective. What sort of amounts are we talking about? To what extent has expenditure in local government grown? In 1969, local authorities spent about £5,800 millions; by 1973 this amount had risen to £8,500 millions; and by 1976 it had gone up to about £13,000 millions, by which time it amounted to some eighteen per cent of the gross national product. In the seven years local government expenditure had risen from about £2 per person per week to about £5 per person per week.

Local authorities have two basic kinds of expenditure: capital and revenue. Capital expenditure is money spent on assets which will last longer than a year and revenue expenditure is money spent on items when the benefit lasts for less than a year, and on such things as salaries. For example, the financing of a new school building would be capital expenditure whereas the cost of heating the building and of the teachers' salaries would be revenue expenditure. Of the £5 per person per week, about £1.25 is spent on capital projects and the remaining £3.75 in current expenditure.

Capital expenditure
To finance capital projects (or, at least, all except small ones) local authorities will borrow money. This they can do either on the stock market or through banks, insurance companies and the like, or from the Public Works Loan Board. This last body was established by Parliament and has money made available to it by the Treasury which it lends to local authorities at fixed rates of interest over a stated period of time. Because the interest rates are fixed, an authority which has borrowed the money knows how much its repayments will be for the whole of the period of the loan, which has obvious advantages to small authorities in particular. Bigger authorities may use the more usual forms of borrowing because they are then able to take advantage of current market conditions.

Local authority capital expenditure has to be judged alongside the claims of all other bodies. If the government feels that there is a need for a cutback in expenditure, it will want local authorities to spend less, and vice versa. Local authority expenditure must, in other words, fit into the overall economic policy of the government. No matter how desirable a vast extension to an authority's housing programme may be, no matter how essential the building of a new school may be regarded, the government will not sanction the projects if it decides that its overall economic policy will be upset. For this reason, the approval of the central government through the appropriate Department or Ministry, is needed for most capital expenditure projects, and all capital expenditure must be within programme totals decided by the government.

As well as paying interest, local authorities are required to pay back the sum borrowed over a stated number of years, up to a maximum of eighty. In the short term this places the local authority at a disadvantage compared with the private firm who would pay interest on the sum borrowed but would not repay the premium. In the long term this balances out as the authority eventually has assets which do not bear interest charges because it owns them completely.

Much controversy surrounds the question of loan charges. Because local authorities borrow over long periods the amount paid in interest is colossal. There are people such as Mr Frank Allaun,

M.P., a member of the Labour Party's National Executive Committee, who advocate loans which are interest-free, or at least heavily subsidised by the government, for some items of local authority spending such as housing. This, he argues, will considerably reduce the cost of building council houses, thus enabling the local authorities to build more and to charge lower rents. As the government would have to borrow the money itself at commercial rates (or to finance the project through inflation, which seems unlikely) what Mr Allaun is in effect asking for, is a Government subsidy for specific capital projects which are regarded as being of high social value so that the projects can be expanded and yet charges, such as rents, remain low. In other words, Mr Allaun is putting forward the concept of social cost instead of the concept of economic cost. It would seem unlikely to appeal to a Conservative Government though it may prove acceptable to a Labour Government – but even then not in times of economic stress, as the Government could only finance such a scheme either by increasing taxation or by increasing money supply and thus fuelling inflation.

Revenue expenditure
Revenue expenditure is met partly from government grants and partly from rates. Sometimes an authority will make a profit from a trading concern which will also be used. These trading concerns cover a surprising variety of activities. Besides the more obvious ones such as housing, transport and baths, there are airports, markets, restaurants, dance halls, theatres and a host of others. All of course have an income to finance their own activities. Many are also subsidised from the revenue expenditure of the local authority. Of the £3.50 per head spent in 1974 under revenue expenditure, rates accounted for just over £1, rents and trading about 0.70p and government grants for the rest.

   Rates are a local property tax. Some properties are exempted from the tax: agricultural land and buildings, churches, charities, parks and open spaces, police properties, most railway and council properties, and Crown properties (though in this last case a 'donation in lieu of rates' is given by the Treasury). Empty property may be exempted at the discretion of the local authority. Those buildings which are rated are called 'hereditaments'. Each hereditament is given a rateable value. This is based on what the rental value of the building would have been at the time of the last valuation (1972) given the nature of the house, at that time and the locality in which it is situated. Put crudely, a big house would be given a higher rateable value than a small one, and one on the edge of a park a higher rateable value than one next door to the gasworks. What is not taken into account is whether or not there is a shortage of accommodation in the area.

The local authority adds up the rateable values of all properties in its area. It can then calculate how much would be received if each ratepayer were charged 1p for each pound of rateable value of his property. From this it is a simple calculation to show how much they will need to charge for each pound of rateable value to meet their expenditure. Let us look at a simple example. Eckshire has a total rateable value of £4 millions. The county council budget to spend, during the next financial year, £3 millions over and above the grants they receive from the government and any miscellaneous income they might have. To raise that amount they need to charge 75p for each pound rateable value (£3 millions divided by £4 millions). This is expressed as '75 pence in the pound'. So, if the rateable value of Mr Smith's house was £150, he would have to pay 75p multiplied by 150 = £112.50. It can be seen from this that the rateable value does not directly tell us how much the ratepayer will have to pay to the authority. We also need to know the rate in the pound that the Council have decided to charge. It is obviously preferable to the ratepayer that he pays only one authority rather than being charged rates separately by two or three councils. Some of the services are provided by the county council and some by the district councils within its area, and a very few by the parishes which form part of some districts. The rates for the county and the parishes are collected by the district councils. The county council makes a rate precept (i.e. tells the other councils how much they should collect on its behalf) which is added to the amount that the district council needs for its own purposes. The districts also add the amount for which the parishes ask. The ratepayer is then told the total rate in the pound. He makes his payment to the district council and they, in turn, pass on to the county councils and parish councils that part which has been collected on their behalf.[1]

The great virtue of rates as a method of taxation is that they are simple and cheap to collect. Council house tenants pay their rates with their rents. Some tenants of houses rented from private landlords will usually pay their rates with their rent and the landlord pays over the rates on their behalf. Other ratepayers pay their rates directly to the council either annually, twice-yearly or monthly over the first ten months of the financial year, as arranged between the ratepayer and the council.

The system has another appeal for governments. They generally accept Corbière's dictum that 'the art of taxation is the art of plucking the goose with the least possible amount of squealing' and one of the ways to keep the squealing to a minimum, they believe, is to raise taxes in a variety of different ways – income tax, Value Added Tax, motor vehicle tax are a few – and a property tax. However, as we shall see later in the chapter, rates are not by any means universally popular, even within the narrow limits of popularity which any tax enjoys. The largest single item in local authority income is government grants. The percentage paid by the Exchequer has increased from twenty-nine per cent in 1967-1968 to thirty-five per cent in 1976-1977. As far as revenue income is concerned, Government grants account for about forty-five per cent. It should be noted that these figures are lower than those often quoted.[2]

Some of the grants are specific grants. In other words, the government makes a payment towards a named service. These services include the police, rate rebate schemes, and the urban aid programmes. After these specific grants are paid, the remaining amount of the aggregate Exchequer aid comprises the Rate Support Grant. This is broken down into three elements: the domestic element, the resources element and the needs element. The domestic element was introduced by the 1966 Act as it was felt at the time that the rate increases being faced by domestic ratepayers were unacceptably high. Indeed, the Minister, Richard Crossman, was of the opinion that rates were a grossly unfair type of tax. He intended to replace the rating system by another means of local taxation and introduced the domestic element as a temporary measure in the meantime. Ten years later, the rating system still survived, and the domestic element amounted to 18½p in the pound. Commercial and industrial ratepayers do not qualify for the domestic element, and there is now a strong body of opinion that considers they are contributing a disproportionate amount to local revenues.

revenues.

If we are to avoid the situation where poor authorities provide ever poorer services because they have insufficient income even to keep pace with inflation and the increasing costs of services, then the government clearly has to make special provisions to help them. This is done through the 'resources' element of the rate support grant, which is paid to those authorities whose rateable resources per head of population are below average. It can be seen from the examples in Table 3.1 that Hampshire received less than three per cent of its income from this element, Lancashire about ten per cent, whilst the sparsely populated, relatively poor county of Radnorshire received over a fifth of its income from the resources element.

Table 3.1. *Income of three counties in 1970-1971*
(Excluding service charges and trading income)

		£,000	%
Hampshire	Specific grants	8,000	13.2
	RSG (i) Needs	30,818	50.7
	(ii) Resources	1,738	2.9
	Rates and balances	20,175	33.2
		60,731	100.0
Lancashire	Specific grants	13,476	9.1
	RSG (i) Needs	77,859	52.4
	(ii) Resources	15,130	10.2
	Rates and balances	41,927	28.3
		148,392	100.0
Radnorshire	Specific grants	495	21.6
	RSG (i) Needs	1,026	44.9
	(ii) Resources	524	22.9
	Rates and balances	242	10.6
		2,287	100.0

The remaining element is the needs element. A basic payment (in 1972-1973 £18.63 per head of population plus £1.44 for each child under fifteen) is made for each authority and to this are added supplementary payments for children under five and old people over sixty-five; for areas which have a very high or a very low density of population; for certain categories of roads; for areas with declining populations; for being within the metropolitan district, and therefore subject to the high costs of that area; and for children at school, based on their age and the numbers per 1,000 population. If we look again at Table 3.1 we see that each authority gets about half of its net income from the needs element of the Rate Support Grant.

That, then, is the system: a local property tax, substantially augmented by grants from the government. How well does it work? Does it allow local authorities the degree of choice which a genuine system of local government should? Is it a fair system? What are the alternatives?

The system considered

A major criticism which is frequently made of the system is that the payment of taxes based on property can be very unfair. The examples usually quoted are, first, the old person who is no longer working but must still pay the same rates as he would if he were still employed and, secondly, the parents of a large family who have to live in a big house but whose capacity to pay taxes is less, not more, than the parents of a small family. The critics point out that it can thus be a regressive tax. Rate rebate schemes have been introduced which can mitigate these problems but introduce, in their turn, the fiercely debated question of means-tested allowances. Whatever the merits or demerits of such allowances, it remains a fact that substantial numbers of people entitled to rate rebates do not take them up – a situation which, the critics claim, reinforces their basic objection. The concept of a property tax is also criticised because it discourages people from improving their property – if they make improvements, the rates go up. Many people feel strongly that a penalty, as they see it, is being imposed for self-improvement.

There seem, at times, to be as many alternatives put forward as there are critics of rates. The favourites are a local income tax, a sales tax, motor vehicle taxation and an entertainments tax. An alternative which is used in some of the German länder is the so-called Gewerbesteuer, which is a local tax on capital and income ranging from one per cent to five per cent of yearly income and two per cent of capital. One of the effects of the tax was to encourage local authorities to attract industry. Another scheme practised in other countries, which is from time to time publicised as being worthy of consideration, is to charge specific fees for such services as street cleansing, refuse disposal and the like. It has never attracted much favour in this country.

The main fault of the present system, from the point of view of local government officers and councillors, is that it lacks buoyancy. The local authorities are making genuine choices only to a very small degree. Although they are frequently criticised for the size of rate increases, the reality of the situation is that almost all of the increase in local government expenditure is accounted for by inflation and the prevention of falling standards.[3] For example, if school population rises by five per cent there will be an inevitable increase in rates without the education system being improved at all. Indeed, Planning Paper No.1, issued by the Department of Education and Science, reveals the fact that only one per cent of the total budget for the education of five to fifteen year olds in 1968-1969 allowed for innovation, the rest went on on-going commitments. So, if standards are to improve income must be more elastic.

In fact, successive governments have tried to help in this matter. The pressures which councillors are subjected to are also applied to Members of Parliament and Ministers. The education lobby is strong nationally as well as locally, as are the housing pressure groups such as Shelter, or Social Services pressure groups such as Age Concern. It would be politically impossible for central government not to have increased the amount given to local authorities in grants. Their efforts to encourage expansion through domestic rate relief has been, as we have seen, less successful as many authorities used the sum to reduce rates, or to finance the whole of the domestic increase in rates, rather than part of the increase which was the intention of the Government. To that extent, local authority criticism rings false. Another criticism of the present system is that the Government control and interference is too great. In fact, this fault is in general more apparent than real. With the exception of the specific grants, the Government gives its grant as a block sum and not to specific projects or to specific services. Many Ministers do seem to assume that specific sums have been allocated because of the way that the calculations of grants are made, but the fact is that local authorities can allocate the Government grant between services as they choose. Any restraints placed on local authorities, or minimum standards set, are matters of policy and not of finance. It is unlikely that, with local authorities now accounting for some eighteen per cent of the nation's resources, any government is going to give total freedom to local authorities to determine overall resources. Indeed there are those who argue that the present block grant system allows too much power to local authorities. The grant's main purpose is to fill the gap between local expenditure and the amount that can be raised through the non-buoyant rating system. However, while it allows for a degree of government control over total expenditure, it does not allow the government to impose its objectives in detail on local authorities. And yet governments are elected having made specific pledges which might not be fulfilled by some local authorities, even though extra resources are provided by the Government.

The Committee of Inquiry into Local Government Finance: The Layfield Committee

In 1974 there were huge increases in rates. While only six per cent of authorities in England and Wales had no increase at all, thirty-eight per cent had increases of more than a half and a further forty-three per cent had increases of between a fifth and a half. The average increase was about thirty per cent compared with the previous average increase of about ten per cent. In some districts the increases were more than 100 per cent. The outcry from the ratepayers was loud and clear: something had to be done about local government finance.

In June 1974, the Secretary of State for the Environment (local government being one part of that vast Ministry's responsibilities) announced to the House of Commons that he intended to appoint a committee of inquiry into local government finance. Its terms of reference were 'to review the whole system of local government finance in England, Scotland and Wales, and to make recommendations'. As is the custom, the Committee has taken the name of its chairman, Frank Layfield Q.C.

Whilst there is little doubt that Anthony Crosland, the Secretary of State, was moved to action by the extraordinary rate increases that year he told the House that 'the Committee of Inquiry will be concerned not with the short-term problem . . . but with long-term issues and the whole nature of the system'. It was the view of the Layfield Committee that 'What the crisis exposed . . . was not simply the weak points in an otherwise sound system, but a collection of financial arrangements whose objectives were not clear and which had never been properly related to each other'. They therefore concluded that what was needed was not adjustments to the present arrangements 'but the construction of a financial system'.

The Committee give a side-swipe to the 1974 and 1975 reorganisation, 'decided without a comprehensive review of the scope that it offered for new financial arrangements. As a result, a variety of two-tier organisations was adopted with diverse and overlapping responsibilities which present serious obstacles to the creation of a financial system providing clear accountability'.

At one level the Layfield report is a technical document proposing a number of changes to the system of local government finance. For example, while it makes a vigorous defence of rates – that is, a property tax – and recommends they be retained as a major source of local government finance, the Committee makes a recommendation that the method of assessing a property's rateable value should be amended to base the calculation on its capital value rather than rent value. Whilst recognising that fees and charges could not finance significantly more of the service, and should not be introduced for services such as education, it did consider there was the opportunity to increase income from this source and recommended that a working party should consider the matter. Other technical recommendations of the Committee include: combining the 'needs' and 'resources' elements of the Rate Support Grant into a unitary grant; abolishing precepting so that each authority would raise its own funds and be seen to do so; having a forum for discussion which could be based on the Consultative Council on Local Government Finance and which would have its own office to promote independent analysis; central government assuming 100 per cent financial responsibility for services where there is no local discretion, magistrates' courts, probation, statutory means-tested benefits, the Metropolitan Police and mandatory student awards. These are but a few of the major technical recommendations and on this level the Committee's work has been most helpful in showing possible improvements to the system of finance. Not all the recommendations will be popular or even acceptable: to change the accountability of the District Auditor *suggests* that local government's record shows it needs stronger outside control than other publicly accountable bodies, a suggestion not backed up by evidence nor indeed opinion expressed elsewhere in the report. Also, some recommendations would give the opportunity for stronger central government control.

However, the main issue raised by Layfield, while having technical considerations, is a political one. Put simply, it is that there must be a choice made about the nature of local government. Should it be more clearly under government control, or should it be given more autonomy? While the Committee leans fairly heavily towards the latter, it says that the decision is for politicians to make and it sets out alternative strategies for achieving either end. What Layfield is in no doubt about is that the *drift* to central control must stop and so too must the situation where it is not clear who is responsible for policy and the financing of that policy. It highlights the fact that improvements to the local government service have in recent years been financed substantially by grants designed to protect the domestic ratepayer from the costs of these improvements.

The cornerstone of the Committee's proposed financial system is the concept of accountability: 'whoever is responsible for spending money should also be responsible for raising it so that the amount of expenditure is subject to democratic control'. But who is responsible? And for what? Part of that pair of questions is easy to answer – the government is responsible for the overall management of the economy and it must therefore be able to ensure 'that changes in public expenditure, including local government expenditure which accounts for over a third of it, do not prejudice its economic objectives.' In practice, there have been considerable difficulties because the financial planning systems of national and local government are quite different in character and there is often confusion about the nature of agreements reached. For example, although representatives of both national and local government reached agreement about the overall growth pattern for 1976-1977, by early summer 1976 (in other words, at the beginning of the implementation of the agreement) the government found that the amount which was likely to be spent exceeded what they had thought was agreed, by £350 million. This was hotly disputed by the local authority associations who claimed their members were sticking rigidly to the agreement. The matter was referred to the Consultative Council on Local Government Finance, a joint committee set up in 1975 to iron out just such difficulties. Before the Consultative Council was established there was no formal procedure for trying to reconcile differences of this sort. However, no one argues with the basic premise that the government must control the overall level of public expenditure.

But what of the rest of those two questions: Who is responsible for deciding the level of provision of a particular service in a particular area? The answer, in theory, is the local authority; yet Mr Fred Mulley spent much of his brief period as Secretary of State for Education and Science (when he was not going round, annoying the education world, claiming that his only powers were in relation to air raid shelters) saying that he had managed to obtain an increase of two per cent in the education budget – and implying that this ought to be reflected in each local authority's budget. Yet clearly it would be a nonsense if each local authority split up its budget in proportion to the amounts in the Public Expenditure Survey. There is no attempt to bring together the budgets of all local authorities to see whether or not they are collectively meeting the government's wishes: the only attempt to aggregate them is in relation to the Rate Support Grant negotiations.

It must be said that there are some quite precise government controls at times. Capital programmes in the education service were, until recently, decided at national level on a project by project basis and even now each local education authority is told how much it may spend in total on its projects in any financial year – unrelated to any other capital expenditure in the rest of the authority's service. Controls can change. Mr Peter Shore, the Secretary of State for the Environment, announced in 1976 that he was going to re-introduce controls of new house building (to give priority to conurbations with really severe housing problems) but at the same time he announced that he wished to introduce a system which would allow local housing authorities much greater freedom to decide their own programmes within capital allocations.

Layfield argues that 'in the absence of a clear dividing line between central and local responsibilities the present confusion can only be ended if the main responsibility for local expenditure and taxation is expressly placed either upon the government or local authorities'. The former can be achieved simply by making the government more formally accountable. But 'the second course would require the introduction of a local income tax to supplement rating as a source of local revenue'. The significance of this is two-fold. In the first place it would swing the balance of finance raising back in favour of the local level – though government grant would still remain the biggest single component of local government finance. Secondly, it would give locally raised finance a buoyancy that rates cannot provide: as incomes rise, so would local authority revenue.

The choice put by Layfield is straightforward enough. Should we head more towards a system of local administration of national government or should we try to reverse the trend? The Committee recognises that any government will 'have its own views about the development of individual services and their priority for expenditure. But it should seek to achieve its objectives by achieving a close understanding with local government rather than by detailed intervention and administrative control. Ministers with responsibilities for services which are administered by local authorities would have to be prepared to accept a less dominant role'.

The forces for postponing the day of the choice are strong. Ministers and ministries who are likely to lose significant political power are unlikely to press for change. A Treasury embattled with economic crisis after economic crisis will seek at this stage to keep tighter control and better consultation, already achieved through the Consultative Council, rather than to introduce a new system which Layfield admits might be difficult to get right straightaway. Local authorities will obviously oppose the formalisation of central control and might prefer to await less crisis-ridden economic times to see other major changes implemented – they may feel that they are more likely to achieve their objectives in calmer times. But change will have to come: on the one hand, to introduce, as Layfield puts it, 'a financial system'; on the other hand to put right the situation where, as one writer notes 'Whitehall has burdened city hall with most of the chores but has retained possession of all the best taxes'.[4]

The councillor and finance

Inevitably, perhaps, money is the major constraint on the activities of the local authority. This is all the truer because of the virtual impossibility of altering the level of expenditure during the financial year. Estimates are fixed, and the rate poundage therefore determined, with effect from the beginning of the financial year in April. Once the estimates have been approved, any expansion of services would require a supplementary estimate; indeed, if the money is not available from contingency funds or balances, a supplementary rate might have to be levied, a course of action which councillors are extremely reluctant to undertake. In fact, apart from the most exceptional circumstances, if no money has been set aside in the estimates for a particular service, then that service will not be provided during that year.

The discipline exercised by the estimates in this way often results in an extremely frustrating period for the councillor – especially the newly-elected councillor, who joins the Council in May, full of bright ideas. He finds that the financial year has just begun, and that he can do very little until estimates time comes round again. The electorate may become equally frustrated and disillusioned, as they vainly expect to see the immediate realisation of all those election promises made so confidently in May. Political control of the Council may have changed hands, but the new majority party has to make do with the estimates bequeathed to them by their opponents.

To obtain a realistic idea of the forces at work, affecting councillors' decisions on finance, and of the relative impotence of councillors for a large part of the year, let us examine a year in the life of a second-tier authority, a District Council, from the May elections onwards. Decisions on finance, of course, in practice affect the overall provision of services by the local authority, and are thus the crucial decisions within the authority. Financial matters will be considered in the first instance by the Finance Sub-Committee; the more important items will then be examined by the Policy and Resources Committee. At the beginning of May, let us assume, a number of seats change hands in the local elections, bringing back on to the Council some former members defeated in earlier years, but also some new councillors without previous local government experience. Control of the council remains with the same party. In the first couple of months there is unlikely to be much activity: the new councillors will be finding their way around, getting to know their colleagues and the officers, and making themselves familiar with the authority's current schemes and difficulties. The existing councillors will at this stage merely be concerned to make sure that the projects planned for the year are in fact going ahead. Thus, a typical agenda for a Finance Sub-Committee in June might be as follows:

1 Election of Chairman and Vice-Chairman: the post of Chairman at least, will always be taken by a leading member of the majority party. The Vice-Chairman will also usually be a member of the majority party.

2 Minutes of previous meeting for confirmation.

3 Work Study – report of the Work Study Officer recommending an incentive scheme for the painting staff of the building maintenance section. As a result of various nationally negotiated pay awards for local authority manual workers over recent years, authorities have effectively been forced to introduce bonus incentive schemes. In many areas the desirability of such schemes has proved to be a recurring topic for discussion at committee meetings, particularly where the short-term costs of bonuses and salaries of the work study staff have exceeded the financial savings resulting from the schemes.

4 Proposed increase in fire insurance premiums for the Town Hall and other council properties.

5 To report terms agreed by the District Valuer for the acquisition of 1 New Street – a property required as part of a town centre redevelopment scheme.

6 To consider sending delegates to various Conferences: for example, Institute of Housing Managers for three days in Brighton, Institute of Works and Highway Superintendents for three days in Weymouth.

7 An application from the District Secretary for a loan under the Assisted Car Purchase Scheme.

8 Report of the Technical Officer: on an application for a grant under the Local Authorities Historic Buildings Act 1962.

9 Report of the Treasurer:
    (a)   a report on the capital budget for the year, detailing the items on which work had already started
    (b)   applications for discretionary rate relief from the Oxfam

shop, the Scouts and Guides, the Y.M.C.A., and the local Archaeological Society

(c)   renewal of bank overdraft facilities

(d)   concessionary lettings of the Town Hall to the local Operatic Society, and to the Arthritic Society

(e)   to write off a debt due to the Council of £7.87 for a special refuse collection

(f)   a report on the computer link with a neighbouring authority. The Council bought time on the computer of a neighbouring local authority. This arrangement was to cause a fair amount of controversy over the next few months, as the Council considered whether it was getting value for money from the arrangement, or whether it should lease a computer entirely for its own use.

10   Official History of the town: to determine the wholesale and retail prices of this booklet.

The agenda items described above are fairly representative of the kind of items the Finance Sub-Committee would have to deal with in the course of the year. Most of these items would not cause political controversy in the sense that the two political parties would not take opposing points of view. From time to time, however, items would appear on the agenda at the request of individual councillors. Such items might be rather different from those customarily dealt with, and might cause a fair amount of disagreement between the parties.

Committee items For instance, at the September meeting, a member of the minority Labour group raised the subject of concessionary bus fares for the old, blind and disabled. The introduction of concessionary fares had incidentally been a feature of the Labour candidates' election addresses in April/May. While there was obvious sympathy from both parties, it was clear that the leading members of the Conservative party were concerned about the possible implications of the scheme on the level of the rates for the ensuing year. Various alternatives to concessionary fares were suggested, but in the end the principle was approved by the Policy Committee, and a detailed report was to be submitted to the next meeting. At the next meeting the Treasurer presented estimates of the cost of a variety of concessionary fare schemes. The majority

party members were still clearly dismayed at the financial implications, and succeeded in deferring a decision yet again by establishing an *ad hoc* working party whose terms of reference included
consultation on the introduction of the scheme with the neighbouring District Council and with the County Council (both
Conservative-controlled, and known to be unsympathetic to the
scheme). By the time of the Finance Sub-Committee's next
meeting, however, the working party had not met; in these
circumstances the Labour group proposed that 'the annual product
of a one penny rate be allocated to meet the cost of a concessionary
bus fare scheme'. The majority group amended this proposal to 'the
annual product of a halfpenny rate'. This was accepted by the Policy
Committee and the Council at its meeting in December, although
the detailed working out of the methods of operation was left to the
working party.

In November the Sub-Committee considered applications which
had been received for grants, subscriptions and donations for the
following financial year. By local standards this particular Council
was extremely generous in its assistance to local organisations, and
this year proved no exception. The total amount of grants was
increased from £2,600 in the current year to £4,200 for the
forthcoming year. Examples of the organisations helped are:

(*previous year's figures in brackets*)	£	£
W.R.V.S. (Meals on Wheels Service)	1,050	(950)
Citizens' Advice Bureau	200	(50)
Old People's Welfare Committee	700	(200)
Road Safety Committee	500	(450)
Five local playgroups (at £40 each)	200	(-)
Rabbit Clearance Society	20	(10)

In fact, virtually all applicants received something from the Council;
the only exceptions being the local Spiritualist Church and the
Migraine Trust.

In November, the Sub-Committee also undertook its annual
financial review of the Council's establishment of staff. A number of
new posts were created. The Sub-Committee agreed to the
appointment of an additional Public Health Inspector, a decision
largely influenced by the proportion of older buildings within the
Authority's area, and the resulting need for both Slum Clearance
schemes and Improvement Area schemes. An additional post of

Building Inspector was also created. This was justified on the grounds of the considerable increase in both commercial and residential development that was expected, and the increased priority placed on the Building Inspectorate functions of local authorities by a recent court case in which a local authority had found itself liable for several thousand pounds in damages. A number of regradings were also made, and certain changes were made in car allowances for various members of the staff. This annual review of the establishment is customarily a fairly straightforward meeting, with little division of opinion. On this occasion, however, one proposal did cause a vote on party lines. The Conservative Government was passing through Parliament a Housing Finance Bill imposing certain duties and restrictions on local housing authorities. This Bill was being bitterly opposed by the Labour Party both locally and nationally. When, therefore, a proposal came before the Sub-Committee to appoint a new member of staff to implement the provisions of the Bill (prior to the Bill becoming law), the proposal was passed only by the Conservatives using their majority on the Sub-Committee.

Another item which caused some disagreement, although this time to some extent cutting across party lines, was also discussed in November. The Mayor wished to lead an official delegation to the daughter town in the USA, and was hoping for financial provision to enable certain members of the Council and certain officers to undertake the visit, and also to buy a gift. Most of the Labour members and some Conservatives were strongly opposed to the spending of public money on international travel for councillors. However, in spite of a certain amount of Labour opposition, funds were allocated for a gift and to meet the expenses of the Chief Excutive and the Macebearer. (The Chief Executive later withdrew from the trip.) Interestingly, the strongest support for the Mayor came from the senior Labour member, very much a traditionalist on this kind of issue.

During the remaining months, the Sub-Committee dealt with a number of technical issues worthy of some comment. Further reports were received from the Work Study Officer recommending bonus incentive schemes for the authority's plumbers, carpenters, and street cleaners and sweepers: all were accepted. At the suggestion of the Treasurer, the principle of *leasing* finance was accepted. The Council had over the years built up a Renewals and Repairs Fund in order to finance such transactions as purchasing new vehicles without having to use up any of the always inadequate capital borrowing allocation. The Treasurer pointed out that the Council could release a substantial proportion of the Renewals Fund for more general use if' the finance for the purchase of new vehicles were to be leased for a given period of years.

Another politically charged item which was considered in the second half of the year illustrates well the tendency of some local authorities to delay decisions on sensitive issues. The Conservative Government had just passed an Act removing from local education authorities the power to provide milk free of charge to primary schoolchildren. The Council we are considering, however, is not an education authority. At the November Council meeting, therefore, the Labour Group proposed that the Council should continue the supply of free school milk, using its powers to spend up to the product of a 2p rate on anything it considers to be in the general interest of its inhabitants. The proposal was referred to the Finance Sub-Committee; the Committee postponed consideration of the motion from its December meeting to its January meeting in order that the legal position could be thoroughly examined. In January, the Conservative group carefully avoided any discussion on the *merits* of the proposal, but instead suggested that enquiries be made of the local education authority, the County Council, as to whether, if the District Council decided to go ahead with the scheme, the County Council would cooperate by making distribution facilities available at the schools. The reply was received in time for the April meeting of the Sub-Committee. The Chief Education Officer said that he could not recommend the scheme to the Education Committee. The Labour Group, taking advantage of the fact that two leading Conservatives were away in America, succeeded in repeating the request to the County Council on the grounds that the decision was one that should be taken by the Education Committee, by elected representatives, and not by an officer.

It is noteworthy that throughout this examination of the issues dealt with by the Finance Sub-Committee over the year, virtually no decisions taken involved additional costs in the current financial year. Where decisions involving expenditure were taken, these all referred to the forthcoming year or still further in the future. This illustrates clearly the constraint exercised on councillors by the estimates for a particular year once they have been passed. The process of drawing up the estimates, therefore, is a crucial process in the policy making of the Council. We can now turn to a consideration of this process in our Council.

Estimates The process can be conveniently divided into two sections: capital estimates and revenue estimates, as outlined earlier in the general discussion of finance. The capital estimates are dealt with in the December or January prior to the beginning of the financial year in April.

During the year individual councillors may have suggested pet schemes of their own – a councillor suggested the damming of a stream that runs through the ornamental gardens, and is usually dry in summer, so that there would be a constant supply of water; a councillor, the Chairman of the local Bowls Club, suggested the building of public conveniences near the bowling green, so that he and other players would not have to interrupt their game for so long. Councillors may have put forward bright ideas originating with members of the public or local societies. During the year, the Council had held a very successful historical exhibition, and as a result it was proposed that the Town Hall cellars (used to imprison Protestant martyrs in the 1550s) be renovated to house a permanent exhibition; the Archaeological society wanted the 150th anniversary of an inhabitant of the town who had discovered dinosaur bones in the locality, to be commemorated by the erection of a memorial, preferably a life-sized dinosaur. The party groups may have put forward proposals to implement various aspects of their policy – the Labour group was pressing for the building of community centres on the various council estates. The officers of the authority will have noted repairs that they consider urgent, e.g. the open-air swimming pool was losing a considerable amount of water each day, and needed a new 'skin'. The officers may indeed have put forward their own pet schemes, such as a considerable increase in the number of greenhouses for the Parks Department. There will also be continuing commitments: schemes, already started, involving expenditure over a number of years – the purchase of properties required for town centre redevelopment. At estimates time, all these proposals will be brought together and the councillors will have to choose their priorities.

Very soon the Council finds its freedom to decide the extent of its capital programme extremely limited. As we have seen earlier, central government as part of its general control of the economy, restricts local authority capital spending. Capital schemes are divided into two sections – 'key sector' schemes, and 'locally determined' schemes. The key sector covers such local authority activities as council house building, educational building, etc., in general, the most politically sensitive areas for which the Minister will want to claim credit. As far as our second-tier authority is concerned, the key sector is limited to housing; the housing accounts are selfcontained, and as such are not included in this particular chapter. It is however worth reminding ourselves, in passing, that the procedure followed in a key sector scheme is for the local authority to submit its plans to the relevant Government Department. If they are approved – and the physical details, such as size of rooms, numbers of power points, and so on, must be approved – the local authority is granted loan sanction, permission to borrow the necessary funds.

All other schemes, including the main bulk of the proposals before our Council, form part of the locally determined sector. The procedure here is that the Government allocates borrowing powers of a certain amount to each County area, say £2 million to East Sussex. The District Councils within the area then agree between themselves and the County as to the individual allocations for each authority. Our Council finds itself with £86,023 for the coming financial year. This system does enable the Government to maintain a firm grip on local authority spending, while allowing local authorities freedom to determine their own priorities within the allocation. In practice, on the other hand, the system has been described as 'a great deal of freedom to spend very little'.

So how does this Council go about deciding how to spend its £86,023? The procedure here is for each Committee to select its priorities from all the various proposals before it. At this stage, therefore, many of the bright ideas mentioned earlier disappear altogether. All the Housing Committee's proposals came within the key sector; the remaining Committees determined their priorities as follows:

Policy and Resources Sub-Committees:	£
Land and property acquisitions	60,000
Donation to Squash Club for new courts	4,000
Town Hall – improvements to kitchen	30,000
	94,000

Health and Planning Committee:	£
West Street car park	4,000
East Street car park	16,000
Coast works	40,000
	60,000

Amenities Committee:	£
Swimming pool repairs	20,000
Northern playing field	4,000
Eastern playing field	7,000
Greenhouses	4,000
Bowls Pavilion conveniences	3,600
Riverside walk	4,000
	42,600

Thus, the total of 'priority' proposals amounted to £94,000 plus
£60,000 plus £42,600 which equals £196,600. It now fell to the
Policy Committee to take the uncomfortable decisions as to which
items should be excluded. It was soon very apparent that the
Committee had absolutely no freedom of manoeuvre. The swimming pool would have to be closed permanently if it was not
immediately repaired, the sites for the car parks were derelict and
eyesores, and the playing fields were part of an existing programme
of work for levelling and sowing. This left a sum, which would
almost certainly prove completely inadequate, for land and
property acquisitions necessary to continue with the town centre
redevelopment. Thus, the final capital programme recommended
to the Council by the Finance Committee was:

	£
Swimming pool repairs	20,000
Playing fields	11,000
Car parks	20,000
Land and property acquisitions	35,023
	86,023

These figures show very clearly how central government control of
local authority borrowing imposes a rigid straitjacket on the wishes

of local councillors, who find themselves in the position of being unable to proceed with schemes that they would really like to see implemented.

Rates Do they have more freedom when they turn to the revenue estimates? In January the Council accepted a recommendation from the Finance Committee that the total rate poundage for the forthcoming year should not increase by more than eighteen and a half per cent. The intention was that this would provide a guideline for committees when they came to consider their revenue estimates. The size of the increase, and the fact that debate in the Committee had centred on whether the increase should be eighteen and a half per cent or twenty per cent, indicates that the Council recognised that considerably increased expenditure was inevitable. One of the main reasons for this was that the County Council's proposed estimates for the forthcoming year had already been published, and were shortly to be confirmed. The District Council has no control over the expenditure of the County Council, but it does have to collect the rates on behalf of that authority. A large increase in the overall rate was therefore inevitable when the County Council announced that their rate would rise from 35.2p in the pound to 41.7p in the pound.

The District Council, as the rating authority, invariably takes the blame from the public for any increase in rates. The overall rate for the current year had been 50.5p, made up of 35.2p for County purposes and 15.3p for District purposes. Now, before the District Council had considered probable increases in its own rate, rates would increase by 6.6p for County purposes alone. If the Council were to keep within the overall rise of eighteen and a half per cent on which they had decided in January, the overall rate must not increase by more than 9.3p: this meant that the district rate could only therefore increase by 2.7p. In financial terms this meant that district expenditure could only increase from £1,004,000 to £1,181,000. Could the District Council keep its expenditure within these limits?

Each committee considered its own estimates, starting from drafts which included provision for as many schemes as possible (including some of those that had not been included in the final capital programme). As presented, the draft estimates were as follows:

Committee	Net expenditure	Increase over current year	Percentage increase
	(£)	(£)	
Amenities	240,000	100,000	71
Health and planning	650,000	200,000	44
Policy and resources	540,000	156,000	41
(Contingencies)	40,000	10,000	33
	1,470,000	466,000	46

An increase of this kind in the Borough Budget was not acceptable on political grounds. The majority Conservative group were only too well aware that five weeks after the new rate demands were sent out, they were due to defend sixteen council seats. If eight of those seats were won by the Labour Party, control of the Council would pass from the Conservatives to Labour. There was thus a great deal of pressure within the Conservative group to keep the increases as small as possible. The Labour group on the other hand, with a rather stronger belief in the virtues of municipal enterprise, was concerned to make sure that an adequate provision, and if possible, expansion, of district services took place. Both parties were, however, agreed that an excessively large increase in the rates would cause hardship to many ratepayers.

The next stage was for the Chairman and Vice-Chairman of each of the Committees to consider what items could be deleted from their estimates, and to recommend accordingly to their Committees. The Health and Planning Committee deleted £160,000 allocated for repairs and improvements – in spite of warnings from the Technical Officer that this could cause considerable problems and even greater expense in the future. This reduced their estimate to £490,000: a nine per cent increase. The Amenities Committee removed from their proposals a number of items, including several which had not found a place in the capital programme, but their proposals still amounted to £196,000: a forty per cent increase. It therefore fell to the Finance Sub-Committee to consider its own estimates, and to make reductions in the other Committees' proposals so that the Council's target rate of increase should not be exceeded.

From Policy Committee's estimates they deleted £40,000 for building maintenance and improvements to the Town Hall and £6,000 for Town Hall furniture and fittings; from the Health and

Planning Committee they removed £16,000; and from the Amenities Committee they took £12,000: not from any particular item, but spread over the whole range of its activities, principally from maintenance costs. Having reduced the proposals by approximately £74,000, they found themselves unable to make further cuts. The estimates, as recommended to the Policy Committee and the Council by the Finance Sub-Committee, therefore, read as follows:

Committee	Net expenditure	Increase over current year	Percentage increase
	(£)	(£)	
Amenities	184,000	44,000	31
Health and planning	474,000	24,000	6
Policy and resources	494,000	110,000	29
(Contingencies)	40,000	10,000	33
Total	1,192,000	188,000	18.7

The Council had, therefore, just failed to limit the increase in the rates to eighteen and a half per cent. A budget of £1,192,000 implied a District rate of 18.2p – an increase of 2.9p. Added to the County rate, this meant an overall rate of 60p – a total increase of 9.5p or 18.8 per cent. Why had the Council, in spite of strenuous efforts, been unable to meet its target? Points made by various speakers in the Council debate on the estimates illustrate the reasons.

The Chairman of the Finance Sub-Committee, in moving his Sub-Committee's recommendation, wanted to stress that he considered ratepayers were getting value for money. He pointed out that the ordinary householder – the domestic ratepayer – would not be paying the general rate poundage of 60p, but would instead be paying a rate of 49.5p. As we saw in the general section on finance, the Rate Support Grant consists of three elements: the needs element, the resources element, and the domestic element. The domestic element is the only part of the Grant paid to district councils and is specifically for the purpose of reducing the rates payable by house-holders, as opposed to commercial or industrial ratepayers. In the year we are examining, the domestic element amounted to 10.5p per domestic ratepayer.

He did not attempt to explain the increases in the County Council's estimates, merely commenting that the County Council was experiencing exactly the same kinds of difficulties as the District Council. The major cause of the increases was felt to be nationally negotiated wage and salary increases, over which, of course, the Council had no control. Salaries alone accounted for one-third of the increase. Wage increases for manual workers were responsible for much of the remaining increase. The Council had, in the course of the year, decided to introduce a concessionary bus fare scheme costing £32,500. The Government's Housing Finance Bill, referred to earlier, made a contribution from the General Rate Fund to the Housing Accounts mandatory: a further £26,000. All the Council's costs had increased: stationery, printing, postage, travel, computer facilities; the Chairman reiterated the point that the Council had no control over these costs. The only way, he felt, that the increase in expenditure could have been kept smaller was by reducing the standard and quality of services provided by the Council, and by overlooking essential repairs. This the Council was not prepared to do. He also drew attention to the lack of 'buoyancy' of rates as a system of raising revenue, which was a particular problem of the district. Income taxes are 'buoyant'. That is to say, as income rises, so does the amount of tax payable and, therefore, the revenue of government. Rates, on the other hand, are not buoyant: the rateable value of a property does not rise over the years, it remains constant until the next revaluation. Revaluations occur at fairly distant intervals: for instance, there was no revaluation between 1963 and 1973. In these circumstances the local authority can only increase its revenue by increasing the rate poundage. The only buoyancy in the rating system occurs when new building and development take place. The rateable values of the new properties add to the total rateable value of the district. The Chairman pointed out that while total rateable values for other districts in the area were growing at about three per cent per year, because of new development, in this district the increase was about one-third per cent since historical and geographical factors prevented much development. This meant, he concluded, that the rate poundage would have to rise faster than in other areas.

The main spokesman for the Labour group expressed dismay that, while there was a substantial increase in the rate, this would not result in a substantial improvement in the provision of services. The increased expenditure, he said, would merely prevent a decline in the standard of service. He pointed out that there were only two items on which the Council had taken a deliberate decision *of its own* to increase expenditure: the increase in grants to local organisations, and the introduction of concessionary bus fares. Otherwise, the Council was simply reacting to events over which it had no control; perhaps unsurprisingly, he blamed the Conservative Government for this state of affairs. The domestic element of the Rate Support Grant was now 2p per ratepayer lower than it would have been under Labour (the Conservative Government had halved the annual increase of the domestic element), the Council had been forced by law to make a contribution to the Housing Account, and nothing had been done to control inflation.

Other speakers picked up this theme. None felt that the rate could be increased further, but many regretted the exclusion of particular items. The increase was described by one Labour member as 'a nail in the coffin of the small businesses of the district'. On the whole, however, the atmosphere was one of frustration, councillors feeling that they had very little real control over the level of expenditure. The highlight of the debate was probably the moment when the first Labour speaker sat down and a Conservative got to his feet to complain about the intrusion of politics into the Council chamber. On which note the financial year drew to a close.

Conclusion Our case study, then, has shown the relatively long period during the year when councillors are unable to take decisions which have an immediate effect on the provision of services by the local authority. If there is concerted political pressure – as there was in this case with concessionary fares – a decision may be taken which commits expenditure for the coming year, but most new items involving expenditure will be deferred until Estimates time. When Estimates time arrives, however, is the councillor really free to take the decisions that he would like to take? Experience seems to suggest that he is not, that freedom of decision at Estimates time is illusory. The Council must maintain a given standard of service, and the cost of providing that standard has increased; schemes are in progress, and cannot be left unfinished; new legislation may have been passed by Parliament requiring increased local authority expenditure; interest charges may have increased, making the capital programme more expensive; some repairs are too urgent to be delayed any further; salary and wage increases may have been negotiated nationally. For all these reasons, increased Estimates and an increase in the rate may be necessary, even before the local councillors have considered any changes they may want to make. As they take their decision, too, councillors will be very aware of the proximity of the local elections. Just five or six weeks after the rate demands have arrived at ratepayers' homes, the electorate may well have the opportunity of re-electing or rejecting at least some of their councillors. A large increase in the rates is extremely unpopular; councillors due for re-election, or a majority group hoping to fight off the challenge of the opposition party and retain control, will therefore be seeking to keep the increase as small as possible. Given that some increase is necessary for the reasons set out above, this means that local freedom is reduced to rejecting all proposals put forward. Indeed, very often the search for economies is carried to such lengths that essential repairs are often deferred, thus storing up trouble and even greater costs for the future. Electoral considerations, rather than technical or practical considerations are paramount. Even finance, so often thought of as a 'pure' subject, is reduced in the end to politics.

4 Polls and politicians

The system of government in the United Kingdom, both local and national, is called representative government. By this we mean that the people living in the various areas of, in the case of local government, the local authority, choose representatives to act on their behalf in those fields of activity for which local authorities are responsible. Representative government simply recognises that it is not possible in modern industrial society for all the people to be consulted on each of the thousands of political decisions which have to be made year in, year out, both by the national government and by local authorities. Instead each adult is given the right to choose representatives to act on his or her behalf for a fixed period. At local level the representatives collectively form the council of the local authority and it is in the council that Parliament invests the powers of the local authority.

Local elections
All people aged eighteen or over have the right to register themselves as electors and considerable effort is made to ensure that all those who are eligible do in fact have their names placed on the electoral register. All registered voters within each ward (which is the name given to the electoral areas in local authorities) have the right to choose the councillors for that ward. Even if a registered voter has moved to a different part of the authority, or indeed to another authority, he retains the right to vote in elections within the area in which he is registered. The person who is elected as councillor is the one who gets most votes even if, in total, more people voted for his opponents than for him. This system has its critics who would prefer to see a system of proportional representation of one kind or another.[1]

The organisation of elections is somewhat different in metropolitan counties, non-metropolitan counties and London. This is strange given that one of the objectives of local government reorganisation was to do away with what Redcliffe-Maud called 'the tiresomeness of local government elections' which required 'a devoted elector to know on which day elections to his particular authority will take place'. Local election patterns still vary from one part of the country to another. County councillors are elected *en bloc* and serve for four years. Thus, those elected in 1977 will not be due for re-election until 1981. Metropolitan district councils elect one-third of the council in every year in which there are no county elections, councillors again serving for four years. Non-metropolitan districts have been given the choice to opt for the same pattern of elections as metropolitan districts, or for whole council elections. In the latter case, those councillors elected in 1976 serve until 1979; after that date, elections will be at four-yearly intervals. Almost all non-metropolitan districts have chosen whole council elections. In London, the elections for both the Greater London Council and the London boroughs are held on a whole council basis.

At top tier level, local elections are usually on a single-member basis – each electoral division returning one councillor. In the GLC, the divisions are in fact also the Parliamentary constituencies. At district level, however, a much more varied pattern can be observed. Within one district there may be wards returning one, two, three or even more members. In some cases, therefore, the voter can be faced with a bewildering array of candidates from the various parties, plus independents. It is no surprise in these circumstances, therefore, that it has been shown there is a distinct electoral disadvantage to those candidates whose names start with letters from the end of the alphabet, and thus conclude the list confronting the voter.[2]

One thing local government reorganisation did was to reduce quite dramatically the number of elected members serving throughout the United Kingdom. In England and Wales the numbers fell from about 34,000 to 22,400 and in Scotland from 3,450 to 1,550. The disappearance of aldermanic benches, the reduction in the number of authorities and smaller councils, between them resulted in fewer than two-thirds of the old councillors finding places on the new councils. A major effect of this was to reduce the average age of councillors. Indeed one study reported in *Local Government Studies* estimated that the average age in one particular council dropped by twenty-five years! There was also an increase in the number of councillors who had an urban background at the expense of those with county backgrounds, which has led to a marked increase in the involvement of the political parties at the expense of the Independent.

Party politics

The question of party politics in local government is argued regularly and the salient points of the argument need to be rehearsed. Those who support party involvement do so for two main reasons. The first is that they see it is through local government many of their economic and social objectives will be implemented and realised.[3] Thus their housing, education and social services policies need the active cooperation of national and local government. National governments provide the framework but their ambitions can frequently be frustrated by local councils who are of a different political complexion. This is particularly true where the legislation is permissive rather than directive. Sometimes the difficulties of framing legislation in terms which are so precise that the intentions of the government must be realised are such that the government in reality depends upon equally committed supporters at local level taking up the spirit of the government's policy. An example is that of comprehensive education where a formula of words which could not be ignored by opponents of a totally comprehensive system of schools has proven extraordinarily difficult to find. The result has been that a small number of councils have ignored carrot and stick alike since 1965 when they were asked to present proposals for implementing a policy of comprehensive education in their area.

The second reason given by supporters of party politics in local government is that it is sensible for people of a like mind to meet together to iron out difficulties so that, when voting in the council or its committees, they achieve as much of what each of them wants as is possible. In other words, a compromise here and another there are worthwhile if it means the achievement of basic policies. The political party to which a councillor belongs will clearly exercise an influence upon him. In so far as he belongs to a party because he agrees with that party's philosophy, he will wish to support the national party's stated policies. Even where he has reservations about party policy, loyalty will probably constrain him to support that policy. This could be seen in 1976 when Labour-controlled councils all over the country found themselves asked by the Labour Government to increase charges for services and allow no expansion of services. Although such actions were directly opposed to the policies on which they were originally elected, councils grumbled but complied. The national party can thus exert some influence on local councillors: the local party will exert very much greater influence. The local party provides the resources in terms of money, publicity and helpers on which the councillors rely for re-election. Councillors will therefore normally take great care not to alienate their local party colleagues. Nevertheless, it is not unknown for Council group policies to diverge from local party policies, particularly on issues which are peripheral in terms of party philosophy, such as the siting of a refuse tip. Such differences are normally patched up as election time approaches. A threatened loss of position or power acts as a great unifier.

The attitude of the party groups towards loyalty in supporting agreed policies differs quite considerably. Labour groups tend to be stricter in the demands placed upon their members – if together they decide on a course of action all members of the group are required to support that decision by voting for it in committee or council.[4] It is by no means unknown for councillors who refuse to do so to have the 'whip' withdrawn, for the councillor to be reported to his local party, and for him to lose the party's official nomination at the next election. It is perhaps a somewhat rigid interpretation of the model rules created by Herbert Morrison, who was probably the most significant local politician ever produced by the Labour Party. On the other hand the philosophical argument for a strong machine was summarised by him: 'A machine without high principles is a machine of no real value. And high principles without an efficient machine constitute but a voice crying in the wilderness. We have to make an efficient machine for a high moral purpose.'[5] Labour councillors would argue that the discipline of a powerful 'whipping' system is perfectly acceptable because it is only by united action that they will effect the changes in society which are their aim. Other parties tend to be somewhat less strict, expecting rather than demanding support for group decisions by group members.

The case against party politics in local government has been argued by Major Henry Haydon, a former chairman of the National Union of Ratepayers Associations. His objections were that:

(a)   The activities of local authorities are basically not of a political nature.

(b)   Local government elections are used simply to keep party machines well-oiled for general elections.

(c)   Candidates are chosen because of their party record rather than ability.

(d)   The electorate loses interest because the debate in the council chamber is meaningless.

(e)   Decisions taken on party political grounds sometimes discourage officers.

(f)   As chairmen are chosen from the majority party, able members of other groups are not used properly.

Major Haydon's first point is, of course, in marked contrast to the viewpoint expressed by those who see local government as essential partners in the realisation of various social objectives. Even where decisions might seem to be more technical, for example, in the areas of transportation, refuse, roads, there is frequently a political dimension in that the lives of various ratepayers will be directly affected and also because schemes in these areas of activity will be competing for scarce resources. Allocating resources is of necessity a political judgement, though not necessarily a party political judgement. It is not clear why the judgement becomes inferior because it is made by a group of like-minded councillors. His second and fifth points are difficult to confirm or deny as it is difficult to find recorded evidence one way or the other. The evidence of experience suggests that there is at least some truth in his third point, though it is less easy to accept the inference that he would wish us to draw – that to remove party politics from local government would improve the quality of councillors. It is by no means true that Independents serving on councils are, or were, universally able. His final point could be true if it is accepted that able men should always be the governors but there is at least some merit in the counter-argument that critics of government should also be able.

Perhaps the most important of Major Haydon's points is his

charge that party politics leads to a lessening of interest by the electorate. It is certainly true that fewer people vote in local elections than in parliamentary elections, usually not more than half the number and, in single by-elections which will not affect control of the council, often not more than one in eight or so vote. Most certainly one of the reasons might be disenchantment with party politics but there may be others. For example, an enormous emphasis is placed by the press on the importance of the central government's role, and in particular the role of the Prime Minister and key Cabinet ministers. Whilst there can be no gainsaying the power and importance of these people, it often appears that it is more from a desire on the part of newspapers to personalise politics (with a consequential reduction in the philosophical and policy aspects), than a thorough understanding of the political system in this country.

If voters really dislike party politics in local government, then one wonders at their remarkable resistance to the electoral appeals by individuals not supported by major political parties. In the 1973 County Council elections, for instance, 639 Independent candidates were elected, compared with 3,750 candidates representing political parties. In urban areas in particular there has always been a marked reluctance to vote for Independents. It may well be that minority parties gain much more support in local government elections than they do in parliamentary elections. Examples are the strong showing by the Liberal party in Liverpool in the first elections after local government reorganisation and the support gained by the Welsh and Scottish Nationalists long before they began to make a breakthrough in parliamentary terms (a path again signposted by Herbert Morrison who had urged creating a strong municipal base before launching into parliamentary elections). These examples reinforce the role of local government in giving a stronger voice to minority groups than our present electoral system permits parliament to do. They certainly do not reinforce the argument that the voter is opposed to party politics in local government. In fact, the intervention of political parties leads to an increased number of contested elections, and thus considerably increased opportunities for participation by the local voter.

Until the 1973 local elections, many parts of the country still had not seen party contests for council seats. In England and Wales in

1967, for instance, of the 22,739 seats available, only 11,822 were contested. In the 1973 non-metropolitan district council elections on the other hand, of the 13,539 seats available, all but 1,556 were contested. Figures from one particular area further exemplify the point. In the East Sussex County Council elections in 1970, fifty-seven seats were due to be elected. In only seventeen cases were contests held, as the Labour and Liberal parties, with only seven and three candidates respectively, made no very positive move to oppose the ruling Conservative party. In the reorganised East Sussex County Council elections just three years later, eighty-four seats were due to be elected. This time there were sixty-eight contests, largely because of the party intervention by the Labour and Liberal parties, with fifty-four and twenty-two candidates respectively, opposing seventy-three Conservatives.

If the intervention of party politics is not the reason for low polls in local government elections, there must be some other explanations for the quite dramatic differences in the number of electors who will vote in general elections and the number who will turn out for local elections. Conclusions need to be tentative if only because vast numbers of people who do not vote claim to have done so when asked by a research interviewer. One example will suffice to make the point: in the 1967 municipal elections in Sheffield thirty-three per cent voted; when asked whether they had voted (and great care was taken with the phrasing of the question so that interviewees would not feel 'guilty') sixty-one per cent of the sample claimed to have done so. Similar claims were made in studies of Glossop and Newcastle-under-Lyme.

One reason given by those who admitted that they had not voted was simply that they could not be bothered, they were the genuinely apathetic. Some people are not able to vote on a particular day either because they are ill or away from home and not eligible for a postal vote.

A very significant reason for voters not turning out is the feeling that their individual vote does not matter. This seems to be particularly true when the winner is almost entirely predictable before the elections. Thus Professor Hampton, in his Sheffield study, found that the poll in safe seats was lower than in marginal seats and fell to fewer than one in five where the Labour candidate had a straight fight with a Communist candidate. More effort is made by the political parties to persuade their supporters that their vote is important in marginal wards and to contact their supporters who have moved house but still have a vote in the marginal ward, and this greater effort is reflected in higher polls. Whether the increase in effort is *fully* rewarded is more open to question.

A further reason for the smaller poll in local elections is that electors seem more ready to use an abstention in the elections to register dissatisfaction with the policies of the ruling party, nationally and locally, than an abstention in a general election. In a sense this is a different dimension to another reason given: that the election 'was only a small one and we only go to the big ones'. Another group of non-voters is that which has a contempt for politicians often expressed in the comment 'They're all the same'. Such contempt seems to be particularly aimed at local politicians.

Space precludes description or analysis of local election campaigns, but it is important to recognise that the publication of election addresses, the canvassing undertaken by the candidates, and other publicity exercises, all serve to inform and educate the local electorate. This costs money and whereas the Independent candidate will need to provide his own funds, the Party candidate can call upon his Party resources, contributed by members and sympathisers. It has been suggested, therefore, that the intervention of parties at the local level has enabled candidates to stand who otherwise could never have afforded to do so.

There are two other important bonuses gained from the involvement of political parties in local government: recruitment and accountability. The first Maud Committee discovered that for many councillors, their interest in local government had developed from involvement in political parties or associated groups. In particular, many Labour councillors had begun their involvement through a trade union, from there had become involved in the Labour party, and later become councillors. If groups put forward policies jointly it is easier to identify those who are responsible for the policies. If promises are broken by a party which has gained power they are unable to shift blame on to other groups. If the policies are popular, the group as a whole will be supported, if unpopular, the electorate has the means to get rid of the governing party and to replace it by another. Thus the public is able to give a clear indication of the sort of policies it is prepared to support. It is not necessary for a party actually to lose power either: if the governing party does badly in an intermediate election but does not actually lose power, they will nevertheless frequently amend their programme in response to what is considered to be the wishes of the people.

To some extent, this analysis of local electoral behaviour presents a more idealistic picture of the intentions and reasoning of the local voter than is justified by the evidence. The analysis has suggested that voters judge councillors, both individually and in their party groups, on their performance, policies, and promises. While this can happen, many voters clearly use local elections as an opportunity to express their opinion of the party in power at Westminster by voting for or against it at local level. The mass media certainly treat local elections as just another opinion poll showing relative support for the national parties. Thus when opinion polls in 1967 and 1968 showed the Labour Government to be extremely unpopular, the Conservatives made overwhelming gains in local elections. In 1971 and 1972, under a Conservative Government, the position was reversed. Many councillors with fine local records were swept away in these landslides, which could certainly not be interpreted as an indictment of their performances. The exceptional candidate or the exceptional local issue may halt or reverse the national trend, but such exceptions are now rare.

Councillors

Who then are the councillors? How are they qualified? Why do they serve? Some of these questions are a little difficult to answer at the moment because there have, since local government reorganisation, been substantial changes in the membership of councils – not so much by recruitment of new blood, though there has been some, as by the removal of much of the old. Before reorganisation the Redcliffe-Maud researchers and others compiled a good deal of information. Councillors tended to be older than average; most were men; hardly any women combined a political life on the council with paid employment though for men it was much less likely that they were out of work than for the male population as a whole; councillors, particularly in county areas, were above average in the number of owner-occupiers, socio-economic group, level of education. Table 4.1. compares councillors with all electors in respect of certain of these characteristics.

Some concern has been expressed that councillors are not fully representative of the electorate. Table 4.1. shows the extent of the discrepancy. Although the table does not give full information in relation to occupational background of councillors, it does show that over half the councillors are employers or professional people, compared with one in eight of electors.

Table 4.1.

Characteristics	All electors (%)	Councillors (%)
Male	45	88
Married	74	87
Employers/professional	13	51
Higher/secondary education	28	54
Property owners	48	67
Under 35 years of age	42	19
Lived less than 16 years in area	31	19
Not born in area	62	63
Work more than 30 hours per week	51	66

Source: Royal Commission on Local Government in England.

Evidence suggests that the position is similar in the *ad hoc* authorities. For instance, members of Regional Health Authorities and Chairmen of Area Health Authorities are intended to help provide the representative element in the provision of the Health Service. Yet their occupational background is clearly unrepresentative, as Table 4.2. shows.

What are the legal qualifications for being elected to a council? The qualifications for election as a councillor are designed to ensure that all those who have a stake in the affairs of the local community – but only those – are entitled to be elected. The qualification for election is to be either a local government elector in the area, or to have lived in the area for the preceding twelve months, or to have one's principal place of work in the area. Thus, somebody who lives in, say, Guildford in Surrey but commutes to work in Islington, London, would be eligible for election to Guildford District and Surrey County Councils, and also the Greater London Council and

Table 4.2 *Appointments made by Sir Keith Joseph as Secretary of State for Social Services*

Occupational background	RHA members	AHA chairmen
Health and allied professions	56	5
Non-medical academic	16	—
Academic	—	3
Trade Union officials	12	5
Manual	3	2
Directors and businessmen	46	
Managerial	16	} 38
Other professional	17	
Retired and housewives	38	22
Farmers and landowners	6	2
Legal	—	13
	210	90

Source: Hansard, 29 January 1974.

Camden London Borough Council; he is of course only entitled to vote in the Guildford and Surrey elections. It should be noted, however, that an employee of a local authority is not eligible for election to that authority. This provision has often been criticised on the grounds that, say, a teacher can hope to gain no more direct personal advantage than can, say, a local estate agent who *is* eligible for election. If a councillor is absent from council and committee meetings for six months, without adequate excuse, his seat is declared vacant and it is not unknown for the former councillor to fight and win the consequent by-election!

We have already noted that political parties and associated groups are major recruiting grounds for councillors. Indeed, the first Maud report showed that seventy-two per cent became involved in local politics because of their association with a political party. There are, of course, other factors that combine to develop an interest: about one in five had a relative already involved and nearly three out of four had friends already involved (though the friends had often become friends because they were members of the same political party). But it is the influence of parties which is all important.

The reasons why people stand as councillors vary, though the biggest divide comes between the reasons given by the councillors themselves and the reasons given by the electors. When questioned by the Maud researchers, councillors tended to give reasons such as the desire to serve society, or to remedy some particular wrong or to advance a particular cause, to represent some group that was under-represented, to serve their party, to continue a family tradition. On the other hand only a third of the electors were prepared to concede such worthy motives: for the majority 'self-interest', 'prestige', 'power' were the motives.

The councillor's role

What are the functions performed by councillors? The following categories can be identified:
(i)   the representative,
(ii)   the specialised policy-maker,
(iii)   the broad policy-maker.
All members perform the representative function, although some do so to a greater extent than others. The representative may see himself as representing a particular geographical area: the ward, the village, the town; he may see himself as representing individual members of the public: the welfare role; he may see himself as representing a particular section of the community: council tenants, landlords; he may see himself as representing a particular organised group: the Chamber of Commerce, the Trades Council. This representative role normally involves dealing with specific cases, reacting to decisions and the way in which council policies affect constituents. Probably three-quarters of councillors generally limit themselves to a representative function. Most of the remainder add to the representative function the role of specialised policy-maker. This implies that they wish to influence council policies in one or two specific areas in which they have a particular interest. Thus, there are councillors who specialise in education or in housing, whose principal ambition may be to attain the chairmanship of the relevant committee. Only a few councillors – probably no more than five per cent – are broad policy-makers, concerned with determining how the council's resources shall be allocated between the various services, and with setting priorities. For a councillor to behave as a broad policy-maker, at least in a large council, it is becoming increasingly necessary for him to be virtually a full-time

councillor and to give up his previous occupation. Thus, Sir Reginald Goodwin, as leader of the GLC, was responsible for a budget larger than that of Israel or of the Exxon Company; Sir Stanley Yapp, first leader of the West Midlands County Council, was responsible for a budget larger than that of Peru. If they are to perform their function as broad policy-makes, as well as their representative function, then their whole efforts need to be devoted to council work. To some extent, this has been recognised by the introduction of attendance allowances for councillors when attending to council business. Even here, however, the rate of allowances has not kept pace with inflation, so that a councillor normally loses more in earnings than he gains in allowances.

Why have councillors anyway? The first reason is that they represent the individuals who make up their constituency or ward. Thus all citizens have the opportunity to have decisions made by the full-time officers challenged and, if appropriate, changed. There is substantial agreement that this task is important and that it is best done by representatives who are responsible to the voters. There is substantially less agreement on the effectiveness of councillors in their other role: the decision-makers.

The major argument used to support the thesis that councillors can have little effect on the decision-making process, is quite simply that the issues are too complicated for the part-time amateur to have the time or skill to consider them in detail. Some administrators seem openly contemptuous of the capacity of councillors not only to influence, but to influence wisely. For example, in the interviews recorded in *County Hall* by Maurice Kogan and Willem van der Eyken, one of the Chief Education Officers says that councillors get in the way of the planning process in which elections are an interruption and elsewhere that 'a CEO knows his area, knows its educational and other needs much better than any lay councillor is likely to do'.[6] Are these charges valid? One at least is not. There is no reason whatsoever to assume that an education officer understands the 'other needs' of his area better than anyone else. No more will any other of the specialist officers have a better understanding of the area's needs outside their immediate field of activity. Do the officers then understand the specialist 'needs' of the area better than the councillors? The answer to that will really depend on what is meant by 'need'. If what is meant is an understanding of the quantitative need – number of schools, number of houses, number of old people needing to be helped in a number of different ways – there is no reason to suppose that the statement is not true. But if what we mean is qualitative need the answer is less obvious. For a start, each service is in competition with the others for resources. Thus, whilst the education officer might know what the need of his area is in terms of pupil/teacher ratios, equipment allowances and so on, these needs must be judged against the needs of the area not only for other education facilities but for old people's welfare officers, housing maintenance and repair men, street lighting engineers and so on. Whilst the decision as to the allocation each service should have could be done by an administrator, it is rarely argued that this transference of resource allocation from the control of those answerable to the public would be justified.

The implication that the use to be made of the allocation should be the prerogative of the officer also has weaknesses. What the CEO is arguing when he decries elections getting in the way of the 'planning process' would seem to be that there is a 'right' way of organising the education service and if only the officers were allowed to plan resources efficiently we would have a better service. But is that true? If it is true it means that administrations are sensitive to the changing aspirations of the people at large and are also prepared to make significant changes in direction should the need arise. The evidence of experience suggests that, notwithstanding significant exceptions, on the whole administrators take the route least likely to cause any major upheaval. Councillors, on the other hand, will be prepared to introduce very significant changes at a more rapid pace than administrators might recommend. This is particularly true in spheres of activity where the parties have national policies which they are pursuing. Comprehensive education, housing finance, development of social service facilities, all provide examples of changes brought about at a pace and in a direction determined by politicians. Whatever the quality of individual councillors there is substantial evidence which shows that the collective knowledge of an area and its aspirations do add a significant dimension to the quality of decision-making in local government; a dimension which makes it local government rather than local administration.

If the political changes were too rapid or alternated at regular intervals, there would be merit in the argument that the development of local government services would be impeded. No service can respond to rapid changes of direction and be efficient. In reality, this is not what happens. Most development occurs at a steady pace but the role of the politician is to decide when the pace is too slow or too fast or when the path being followed is the wrong one. The politician obliges the administrator to reassess at regular intervals the policies being pursued and to open the review to more public inspection. It is thus that the public should influence local government to produce a service in tune, so far as it is possible, with their demands.

There is, however, worrying evidence that the representatives' views of priorities and major policies do not always accord with those of the electors. One of the difficulties that the public representative is, almost inevitably, faced with is how to find out what his electors' (or even his supporters') opinions are. His first problem is that of time: Hampton's Sheffield study showed that the average councillor spent about forty hours per month in council and committee meetings. This may well have increased since local government reorganisation. In addition, he will sit on other bodies such as school governors, area health committees, water boards and the like, and he will attend conferences and meetings of his party. For chairmen of committees there will be substantial contact with principal and chief officers.

His second problem is that the constituents with whom the councillor does make contact are not a representative sample but are, on the contrary, self-selected. Hampton's study showed that councillors did make considerable efforts to be available to their constituents, spending nearly twelve hours a month on electors' problems alone. Whilst only six per cent of councillors had made no contact with electors over the period, some twenty-three per cent had had between twenty and forty-nine contacts and thirty-four per cent had had fifty or more. Labour councillors gave this aspect of their work much more significance. That this is important and best done by councillors was emphasised when the question 'why have councillors anyway?' was first posed. The danger is to assume that such a self-selected group as those who contact a councillor, either because they have a grievance or because they form part of a pressure group, can help a councillor decide what the important issues are, in the opinion of the voters at large.

Hampton asked councillors and electors what the most important local issues were at the time of the survey. The councillors were in no doubt that the two major issues as far as they were concerned were housing and education. The voters agreed about housing but were much more concerned about redevelopment than comprehensive education or the general provision of education. Most significant of all was the difference in importance attached by the two groups to roads and traffic. Fewer than one in five of the councillors thought that this matter was one of the three most important local issues whilst over half of the electors did. In part, the difference can be explained very simply: a councillor who knows that much the biggest service provided by local government is education will accord it a high level of importance, while the voter is much more likely to accord importance to those factors which are having direct impact on him, especially if the impact is adverse. Bad housing, congested roads, poorly conceived redevelopment schemes will rank very high on the list of issues to be regarded as important by those who suffer from one or more of them.

For the councillor, the difficulty is how to respond sensitively to the changing needs and aspirations of the electorate. Hampton argues that 'periodic elections are too blunt an instrument to register opinions on individual topics and the councillors should not assume too readily that they embody the commonweal'. In this, Hampton is reflecting a major criticism made by the Skeffington Committee in their report *People and Planning* that methods of consultation and finding out the real public will were inadequate. The process of consultation will be discussed further in Chapter 6.

The demands of the services are such that full-time officers must support and advise councillors and implement, with substantial discretion, the policies decided by the council and its committees. Traditionally, these officers have been 'profession-based' rather than 'local-government based'. In other words, an officer in the education service would see his development mainly, if not entirely, within the education service rather than in local government as a whole. This is particularly true at the higher levels but is substantially true at medium levels of management. It has usually been the case that senior officials in service departments will have had experience 'in the field'. So senior education officers, for example, will usually have had teaching experience.

The 'professionalism' of local government officers reinforced the division which has long existed between the different services of each local authority. Bains commented that 'as new functions have been given to local government to perform, so new "professions" have grown up, each with its own professional body to develop and improve the skills of its members, but often becoming increasingly concerned with the status of that particular profession in relation to others'.[7] Bains and most of the other committees appointed to review local government in various ways, have argued the blurring of the lines somewhat. There seems little prospect that the 'professional' will disappear altogether – and indeed it seems likely that he will retain sole rights to the chief officers' job in each service in most authorities, but there is a small and increasing recognition that many of the jobs at all levels demand not the 'professional' skills brought by former social workers, teachers, housing managers, engineers, lawyers, and so on, but managerial skills which can be used by all services. It seems likely that the two types of local government officer will continue to exist. The one emphasising the service base of local government, the other emphasising the need for what is now termed the corporate management approach to providing a total service in the area.

5 Internal relations

Within the local authority, the relationships that matter are those between councillors, between officers and between councillors and officers. Although some attempt can be made to distinguish between the roles of the councillor and the officer, inevitably there is considerable overlap. As with so many other aspects of local government, practice can vary considerably from one authority to another, depending on variables such as type, size, political involvement and local custom.

Staffing

Since the early 1960s in particular, there have been a series of reports and recommendations aimed at improving the efficiency of the internal workings of local authorities. The Mallaby Committee on Staffing in Local Government (1966) emphasised the need for the local government service to reorganise its pattern of recruitment so as to take advantage of the increasing numbers of young people benefiting from higher education; the need to provide a coherent career structure for the lay administrator; the need to establish, within each authority, responsibility for the training function; and the need for a Local Government Training Board. The LGTB was established shortly after the Mallaby Report and has done much to revolutionise local government staff training procedures with its training recommendations for groups varying from roadworkers to senior administrative staff, with its support for courses ranging from induction courses for junior entrants to management courses for Chief Officers, and with its levy/grant system which led to the employment of Training Officers in most large authorities and a more equitable sharing of the burden of training costs.

The Mallaby recommendation concerning the need for a coherent career structure for the lay administrator in local government illustrates an interesting contrast between practice in local government and practice in the civil service. In the civil service, at least prior to any positive implementation of the relevant proposals of the Fulton Report, the top posts within government departments have invariably been held by lay administrators, the 'generalists', members of the former Administrative class, while the professionally qualified scientists, engineers, etc., have not held positions of major managerial status. In local government, on the other hand, the position has been exactly reversed. Each department has normally been headed by an officer holding the relevant professional qualification, Solicitor, Treasurer, Planning Officer, etc. In local government it has been extremely difficult, if not impossible, for the general administrator to obtain a post as Chief Officer or Deputy.

The Maud Committee

In 1967 the Maud Committee on Management in Local Government published its report. While considering its recommendations, the Committee had taken note of the experiences of one or two authorities that had been experimenting with their management structures. Newcastle, for instance, had replaced the traditional post of Town Clerk with what came to be referred to as a 'City Manager', and had recruited to fill this post Frank Harris, a former executive with the Ford Motor Company. It was hoped that Harris would be able to inject into the administration of the city the more streamlined techniques of industry. Some of his innovations are mentioned below, but it is interesting to note that Harris left Newcastle in 1969 to return to industry. He is quoted as commenting on the difficulty of establishing precise objectives for local government, as opposed to the situation in business which he saw as dominated by the profit motive. A much smaller authority, Basildon, had acted along similar lines to Newcastle in appointing a Town Manager, David Taylor, a Coal Board executive, whose previous local government experience was as an elected member. Although these two attracted the most publicity, other councils were also making appointments along similar lines.[1]

The Maud Committee was clearly impressed by these developments for they recommended that all authorities should appoint one officer, normally the Clerk, as undisputed head of staff, and that this officer should not necessarily be a lawyer as Clerks traditionally were. The Committee's reasoning was that local government had been suffering from departmentalism and disunity. The conventional situation was that each department was headed by a chief officer, each chief officer had equal status, and the Clerk was simply one chief officer among several. In many authorities, chief officers were jealous of their status and saw it as bolstered by the size of their 'empire'. Coordination of the activities of the authorities was made more difficult by the fact that no one officer had overall responsibility. By convention, coordination had often become a duty of the Clerk, whose department serviced all the various committees, but this coordination tended to be more by way of informing different departments of what was going on rather than by way of laying down an overall strategy for the authority. The difficulties of coordination were enhanced by the large number of departments that existed in many cases. Maud found these averaged fifteen in the top tier authorities. In one extreme case there were thirty-five, with three separate Engineers' Departments. The years leading up to reorganisation saw an increasing number of councils adopting the Maud suggestions to reduce the number of departments and appoint one officer as overall head of staff.

The Bains Report

These developments, however, became almost universal on the reorganisation of local government. Very influential in this context were the Bains Report in England and the not dissimilar Paterson Report in Scotland. The Bains Report – the Report of the Working Group on Management and Structure for the New Local Authorities, headed by Malcolm Bains, then Clerk of Kent County Council – was adopted by a very large number of authorities. Rather uncritically, and perhaps rather unfortunately, it was used as a complete blueprint for management structures.

One outstanding result has been the creation of the post of Chief Executive as head of staff. All local authorities, with the exception of one district council, have made such an appointment. Some idea of the tasks of the Chief Executive can be gained by reading the job specification suggested by the Bains Report:

Job specification for a Chief Executive
1 The Chief Executive is the head of the Council's paid service and shall have authority over all other officers so far as this is necessary for the efficient management and execution of the Council's functions.
2 He is the leader of the officers' management team and, through the Policy and Resources Committee, the Council's principal adviser on matters of general policy. As such, it is his responsibility to secure coordination of advice on the forward planning of objectives and services and to lead the management team in securing a corporate approach to the affairs of the authority generally.
3 Through his leadership of the officers' management team he is responsible for the efficient and effective implementation of the Council's programmes and policies and for securing that the resources of the authority are most effectively deployed towards those ends.
4 Similarly he shall keep under review the organisation and administration of the authority and shall make recommendations to the Council through the Policy and Resources Committee if he considers that major changes are required in the interests of effective management.
5 As head of the paid service it is his responsibility to ensure that effective and equitable manpower policies are developed and implemented throughout all departments of the authority in the interests both of the authority and the staff.
6 He is responsible for the maintenance of good internal and external relations.

At the very least, the implications of this almost universal acceptance of the concept of a chief executive are summarised in this comment in a report from Birmingham University's Institute of Local Government Studies: 'Appointing an officer with terms of reference similar to those in the Bains Report does not necessarily mean that the officer will behave differently from the traditional clerk, but it is symptomatic of the new orthodoxy amongst local authorities which **recognises the need for formal coordinating machinery**'.[2] About half the local authorities have appointed a Chief Executive without specific departmental responsibilities – where he does head a department, it may include personnel services, management services, or public relations, rather than the traditional committee servicing functions of the Clerk. This is an interesting development, particularly in the light of David Taylor's experience at Basildon: originally appointed as Town Manager without a department, he felt himself isolated until he brought the committee clerks under his direct control, only then did he consider that he was receiving an adequate flow of information.

Before turning to the relationship of the Chief Executive with his senior colleagues, it may be instructive to read the following extract from the Diary of a Chief Executive of a District Council. Although the extract does not spell out the precise functions being performed by the Chief Executive, it does indicate the amount of time that is occupied by meetings, formal and informal.

Not so much employment – more a way of life

Monday 14 April
In at 9 a.m. Review of Finance Sub-Committee meeting.
9.30 a.m. Chairman of Administrative Officers' Group came very briefly for regular meeting, as I had to leave to attend a special meeting of the County Chief Executives' Group, to discuss planning liaison. Lunched there with other Chief Executives and then returned to do various jobs of work.
4.30 p.m. Information Officer came to discuss Annual Report and other matters. Left at 7.50 p.m.

Tuesday 15 April
In at 9 a.m. District Treasurer and District Secretary came for regular meeting.
10 a.m. Chief Officers' Management Team, until lunch time.
1 p.m. Working sandwich lunch for newly appointed Chairman's Secretary/Organiser to meet Chairman of Policy and Amenities Committee and Organisers of local Festival and Games Tourney.
2.30 p.m. Policy Committee Call-over.
8 p.m. Meeting with representatives of neighbouring District Council. Left at 11 p.m.

Wednesday 16 April
In at 9.20 a.m. Chief Environmental Health Officer came to discuss Armorial Bearings on council vehicles.

9.45 a.m. Joined a Members' Working Party in the Council Chamber until lunch time.

1 p.m. Lunch with Chairman of Planning Committee and Chief Executive of the County Council.

2.30 p.m. Ratepayer formerly employed at the Bank of England came to discuss the Council's finances – very interesting – he left at 4.15 p.m. Worked at a variety of matters until 6.15 p.m. Performance Review Sub-Committee meeting. Left at 11.35 p.m.

Thursday 17 April

Worked at home until lunch time; in at 2.15 p.m.

2.30 p.m. Staff Communications Seminar: went very well, and a number of valuable points were made which I have since written out and circulated to Chief Personnel Officer and other Chief Officers, for attention. Returned to my office with a Councillor who had taken part in the Seminar, and spent some time discussing office accommodation with the District Architect.

7 p.m. Special meeting of the Amenities Committee. Left at 11.20 p.m.

Friday 18 April

In at 8.45 a.m. Dealt with post. Had intended to attend the special meeting of the Planning Committee on the County Structure Plan but was preoccupied with other affairs, mainly liaison with the District Valuer's Office over the Community Land Bill, and the possible purchase of additional office accommodation, but also with the production of an official list for the Chairman-Elect's use in compiling his Civic List.

12.30 p.m. Working lunch with the Planning Committee.

Attended the Planning Committee meeting on the County Structure Plan for the whole of the afternoon. Returned to my office to deal with various matters, and left at 7.30 p.m.

Monday 21 April

In at 9.30 a.m. Regular meeting with Chairman of Administrative Officer's Group, until 10 a.m. Spent rest of morning on various matters.

2.30 p.m. Meeting, concerning possible uses of disused historic building near the Council's offices, with the District's Senior Planning Assistant and the Assistant County Planning Officer.

3.15 p.m. Made arrangements for various minor works at the

Council's offices, especially to the reception area.
3.30 to 4.30 p.m. Staff interviews.
Then immersed in various tasks, including discussions with Chief Technical Officer and Information Officer. Left at 8.45 p.m.

Tuesday 22 April
In at 9 a.m. Regular meeting with District Treasurer and District Secretary.
10 a.m. Chief Officers' Management Team meeting.
1 p.m. Settled minutes of special Amenities Committee with the District Secretary, visited Council's Law Library, lunch with District Secretary and Information Officer.
2.30 p.m. Recorded an item on Performance Review for BBC local radio.
2.45 to 4.30 p.m. Chairman of Planning Committee, Chief Planning Officer, and Senior Planning Assistant came to settle report on the Structure Plan meeting.
5.30 p.m. Information Officer and a journalist from the local weekly newspaper came to discuss various news items. Left at 6 p.m.
Worked at home from 7.30 p.m. until 4.20 a.m.

Wednesday 23 April
In at 9.45 a.m. Various matters.
2.30 p.m. Adjourned meeting of Performance Review Sub-Committee.
4.45 p.m. Chairman and Secretary of District NALGO Branch came to see me, at my request, in advance of their Executive Committee meeting.
7 p.m. Policy and Resources Committee meeting. Left at 11.15 p.m.

The Chief Executive is leader of the officers' management team. This team will consist of a majority, or all, the chief officers, as illustrated in figures 5.3, 5.4 and 5.5. The Bains Committee sees the management team as performing two principal functions. 'The first is the long term strategic function of considering and advising on what policies the Council should be adopting to cope with changing needs and circumstances and the second the overall management coordinative and progress chasing role.'[3] There are few if any major decisions taken by a local authority which do not affect the areas of responsibility of the majority of Chief Officers. The implications of such decisions for the whole authority need to be considered before they are taken. The Chief Officers are the members of staff who have the required knowledge, experience, and management skills to consider these decisions. The usual practice is that the Management Team meet once a week with a formal agenda, with such other meetings as may be necessary. It is clear that, if the team is to operate successfully, the personalities involved must be compatible, and that the chief officers concerned must believe in the advantages of the system, and not continue to see the activities of the authority from a partial, departmental standpoint.

Committees
So far in this chapter, attention has been paid to the changing style of relationships at officer level. At the same time changes have been taking place in the style of relationships at member level. Once again the Maud Report in 1967 acted as a spur to local authorities to review their structures, although some had already taken action. In Newcastle, for instance, Frank Harris had produced a scheme for a reduction in the number of committees from thirty-seven to eight; this attempt to reduce the number of committees in order to prevent fragmentation of the work of the authority, and in order to reduce the work-load for the individual councillor, was a feature of most of the changes taking place at that time. Bradford, for instance, reduced its number of committees to six, with a corresponding reduction in sub-committees. In that authority, in 1964-1965, a total of eighty-three committees and sub-committees met on 716 occasions; in 1968-1969, this had been reduced to thirty-four meeting on 371 occasions. The impact on the individual councillor in that city was even more striking. Excluding council meetings, he had, on average, attended 129 meetings for a total of 497 hours in 1964-1965; in 1968-1969, he attended twenty-four meetings for a total of forty-four hours.

The purposes of changes of this kind were many: to reduce the time councillors needed to spend on local government work, in order to attract more able representatives and to give them sufficient time to think strategically rather than about details; to enable coordination of the work of the various committees to be more easily implemented; and to allow day-to-day operational decisions to be taken by officers. Most authorities adopting schemes of this kind not only reduced the number of committees, but also the number of members serving on each committee. Furthermore, a central coordinating committee was usually established. Although most councillors grew to appreciate the virtues of the changes, some criticisms were still made, to the effect that councillors were now unable to enjoy sufficient participation in a wide range of council affairs; that too much was left to the chief officers; and that too many decisions were taken by small groups of members, especially the policy committee, without consulting members as a whole.

The reorganisation of committee structures highlighted one major problem in the operations of a local authority: the extent to which councillors, rather than officers, should have an executive role. It has sometimes been said that councillors are responsible for policy, and officers for administration. Local government practice has certainly never aligned itself with that distinction. In the past, only the most minor matters were delegated to officers while committees retained a whole range of executive decisions for themselves. In fact it is impossible to draw a distinction between matters that are policy and those that are administration, one shades imperceptibly into the other; a series of administrative decisions become accepted as policy; only a fairly detailed involvement with a service gives the councillor sufficient knowledge on which to base his decisions. For these reasons, virtually all councils have given executive powers to committees, and, while delegating rather more to officers than was the case in the past, still tend to prefer to delegate to committees.

The alternative strategy is to have a system of purely advisory committees, with the overall management decisions taken by the Policy Committee and the Council. The implementation of those decisions would be the responsibility of the officers. Under this system committees with executive power would merely distort the mechanisms of control within the authority, and, in reducing the range of responsibility of the officers, would be less efficient in so far as a committee is further removed from the task itself. Councillors however have not looked favourably upon the idea of being mainly limited to an advisory, debating role. Unkind critics have suggested that in fact most councillors could not cope with the rather more abstract task of establishing needs and objectives, and are only suited to the consideration of small, concrete details. Most councillors are much happier considering whether the charge for cesspit emptying should be increased by £1 or £2 rather than discussing whether a greater share of the council's resources should be devoted to its housing programme at the expense of its amenities programme.

Committees are the formal machinery by which councillors and officers are brought into contact. Although officers are not actually members of the committees, they are normally free to contribute to their deliberations and guide and advise members. Following the Bains Report, most councils have adopted a system of programme committees together with a central committee and sub-committees. The way in which a council reaches its decisions, and the relative importance of the contributions of members and officers, will depend to a large extent on the number of committees and departments that are established, and on the machinery that is evolved to link the various activities together. This may help us to see whether the council itself views its work as a unified whole, or as a set of relatively unconnected activities. In this context, it is helpful to use the concepts of differentiation and integration.[4]

Fragmentation or coordination?

Differentiation refers to the division of an overall task into various component parts, and is analogous to the idea of the division of labour. The extent of differentiation in a particular local authority can be measured by the number of committees, departments and specialist units that have been established. At the member level, the INLOGOV survey shows that most county councils have between six and ten committees, with eight being the most usual number, and that three-quarters of the District Councils have five or six committees. Typical committee structures are shown in figures 5.1 and 5.2. At the officer level, the survey shows that most county councils have between ten and thirteen departments, and that most district councils have between four and eight. Typical departmental structures are shown in figures 5.3, 5.4 and 5.5. As far as specialist units are concerned, nearly 100 per cent of local authorities have established personnel units; over fifty per cent have also set up separate units for management services and for public relations.

The criteria for differentiation vary rather more from one

Figure 5.1. *Committee structure of a non-metropolitan district*

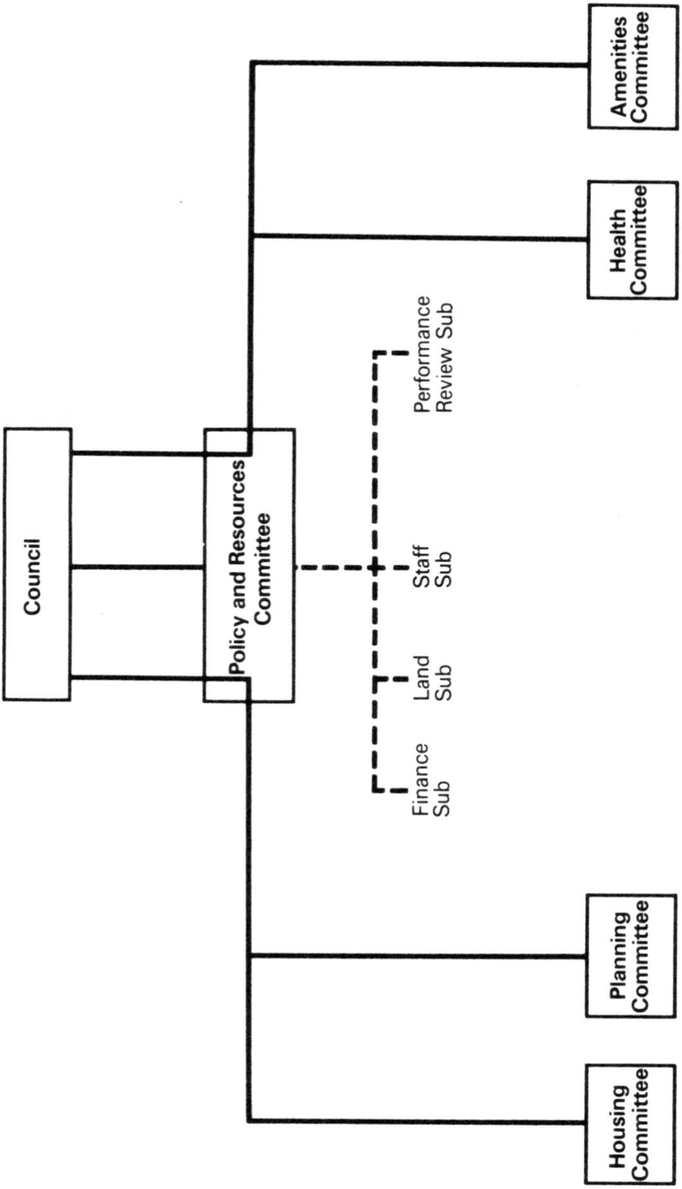

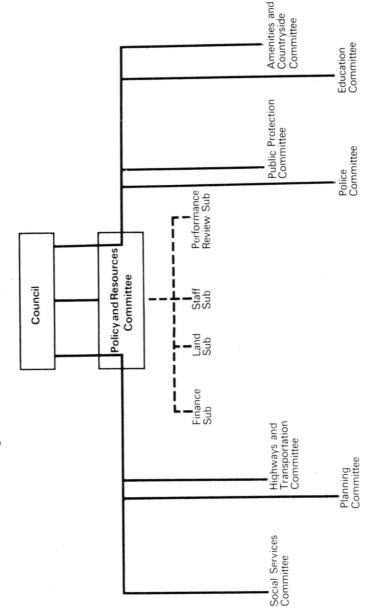

Figure 5.2. *Committee structure of a non-metropolitan county*

Council to another. The most popular criterion has proved to be the 'programme' committee, recommended by Bains, and illustrated in figures 5.1 and 5.2. A programme committee is one that is responsible for a specific sphere of the authority's activity, with its own objectives and programme for meeting those objectives. Over half the district councils have set up all four programme committees shown in figure 5.1; over half the metropolitan district councils have five out of the six recommended in their case. On the other hand, half the county councils have only three out of the six (excluding Police) shown in figure 5.2. An alternative, or addition, to the programme committee is the 'area' committee, where the criterion for differentiation is a specific geographical area: the INLOGOV survey shows that very few authorities have adopted this system as yet. At the officer level, we find that the criterion for differentiation is still very much the individual profession, as illustrated in figures 5.3 and 5.4. The only major departure from the profession as the method of departmentalising the work of local authorities can be seen in the non-metropolitan districts, where two-thirds have established Directorates of Technical Services.

One significant change that has taken place in the last few years emerges from this study of differentiation. Prior to the reorganisation of local government, such a study would have found both more committees and more departments in the majority of local authorities. Furthermore, committees would very often have been organised on a system where each committee matched a particular department. Such a system had the advantages of ensuring continuous political control over the department, and providing the department with a political point of contact for advice and support. On the other hand, it tended to encourage 'departmentalism', competition for resources, and a failure to achieve overall coordination of the authority's work. The survey evidence quoted above shows quite clearly that local authorities have now moved away from the 'one department one committee' system by the establishment of programme committees which will need to draw on the skills of several departments. The criteria of differentiation, therefore, emphasise a conscious attempt at coordination, which leads us to the concept of integration.

Integration refers to the systems used to unite the activities of an authority – to counterbalance the division of labour. The extent of integration can be assessed by the number of central coordinating committees and sub-committees, and the use of similar mechanisms at the officer level. The INLOGOV survey shows that most local authorities agree upon the functions to be discharged at the centre – policy coordination and resource management – but that they disagree on the required number and status of committees. The Bains recommendations shown in figures 5.1 and 5.2 are the usual situation: all but five local authorities in the non-metropolitan areas have a Policy Committee, for instance. However, only a minority have established a Performance Review Sub-Committee. At officer level, discussion has principally been concerned with the question whether certain integrating functions should be based in a department headed by the Chief Executive, and whether all chief officers should be included in the management team. As mentioned earlier in this chapter, sixty-six per cent of Chief Executives do not head a department; where they do, however, the department usually exercises integrating functions such as personnel services. All chief officers form the management team in the majority of district councils, but in the counties the team normally consists of only a majority of chief officers. These situations are illustrated in figures 5.3, 5.4 and 5.5.

Differentiation and integration, then, are methods of analysing organisational structures: the formal network of relationships between councillors and officers. The research carried out at INLOGOV shows that organisational structures are much affected by a number of variables. These are shown in outline in figure 5.6.

Detailed analysis of the research is beyond the scope of this book, but it is important to notice the complex and interacting nature of the determinants of the relationships within the local authority. The size of the authority – the total population, the total area, and the number of councillors – is positively associated with both differentiation and integration; so too, the greater the range of functions that the authority has to perform, the higher is differentiation and integration. The more functions an authority performs, the more likely it is to be involved with other organisations, such as the Area Health Authorities and the Regional Water Authorities; formal machinery will be established to deal with the consequent problems. Explicit policy statements by authorities in favour of corporate planning, and of participation, also have a positive effect on

Figure 5.3 *Departmental structure of a non-metropolitan county*

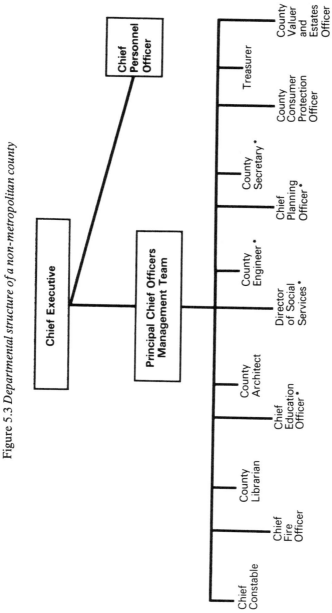

Chief Personnel Officer

Chief Executive

Principal Chief Officers Management Team

Chief Constable

Chief Fire Officer

County Librarian

Chief Education Officer*

County Architect

Director of Social Services*

County Engineer*

Chief Planning Officer*

County Secretary*

County Consumer Protection Officer

Treasurer

County Valuer and Estates Officer

*Members of Management Team

Figure 5.4. *Departmental structure of a non-metropolitan district*

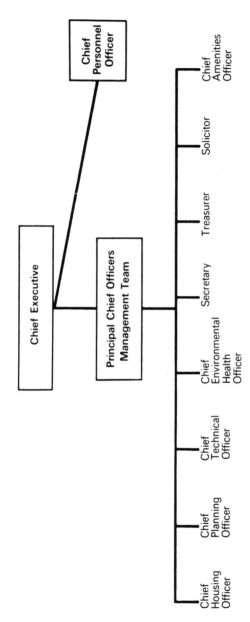

All chief officers may be members of the management team

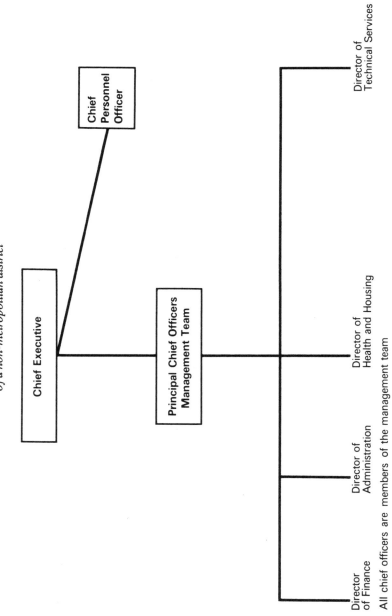

Figure 5.5. *Alternative departmental structure of a non-metropolitan district*

All chief officers are members of the management team

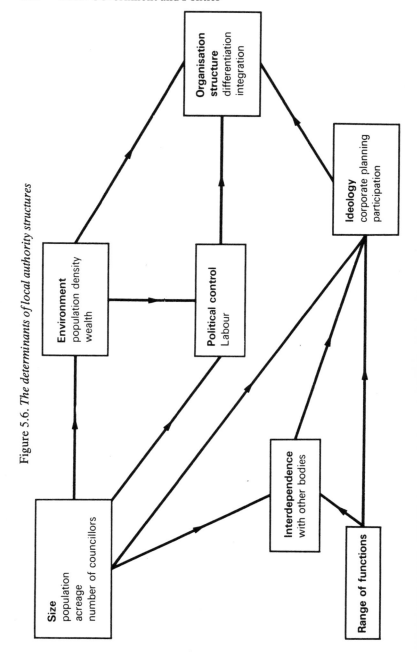

Figure 5.6. The determinants of local authority structures

structure, as does political control by the Labour Party. Interestingly, political control other than Labour appears to have no particular impact on structures.

Political control and ideology can be seen as two filters through which the other variables pass in order to affect structure. They are thus of major importance in determining relationships within the authority. While political control is primarily concerned with the decisions that actually result, the two ideologies under consideration – belief in community planning and belief in participation – are primarily concerned with *how* the decisions are taken.

Corporate management

Corporate planning or corporate management are phrases that cannot be avoided when discussing local government today. The Bains Committee emphasised the desirability of the corporate approach, and all local authorities now pay at least lip-service to the idea. The management function is essentially a continuous process, and can be summarised as follows: 'deciding what is to be done, and getting it done through people'. More helpfully:

(a)   establishing the needs of the area
(b)   setting objectives
(c)   defining policy
(d)   developing plans
(e)   testing plans
(f)   formulating the programme
(g)   implementing the programme
(h)   monitoring
(i)   evaluating success
(j)   reviewing objectives.

This process can be applied to each programme area individually, but the essence of corporate management is that the objectives, policies and plans are formulated from the point of view of the local authority as a *whole*. The Policy and Resources Committee, and the management team, should not be a collection of partial interests, an occasion for the resolution of conflicting claims; rather it is seen as an opportunity to weld the various functions of the council into a unified scheme within the context of the council's strategic objectives. It is fair to say that many local authorities, in spite of their establishment of Policy and Resources Committees and of management teams, do not practise corporate management in the sense described above. A study of the Agendas for Policy and Resource Committees will show that many simply consider the reports of Programme Committees and exercise a coordinating function: not formulating policy but approving or rejecting it. Furthermore, Programme Committee Chairmen usually sit on Policy Committees and tend to see their role as spokesmen for their Committees, rather than as examining suggestions from the point of view of the authority as a whole.

Corporate management is sometimes described as being a management process that is not affected by political control. In fact, this is not the case. A number of councils have adopted one-party Policy Committees: it is perhaps surprising that the number is so few. Although Bains specifically argued against one-party committees, the logic of corporate management might well lead to the exclusion of minority parties. Corporate management involves agreement as to the needs of the area, and as to the objectives, policies and plans to be followed. On a wide range of issues crucial to the local government service, the philosophical bases of the political parties are so far apart that agreement is not possible. Such differences can occur over the implementation of that strategy in particular fields. In any event, the corporate approach, it could be argued, will be seriously weakened if the management of the authority, the Policy Committee, contains members who disagree with the whole basis on which the council is operating. Those authorities that have made provision for minority party representation have done so largely in order to introduce a critical note during the policy formulation stage rather than later, and in order to keep the minority informed. This has proved particularly useful where elections have resulted in a change of political control on the Council.

It must be remembered, however, that local authorities are not the House of Commons. In many local authorities, control by one particular political party is a permanent feature. In this context, it is worth noting that corporate management may be especially suited to a particular political outlook. Corporate planning in fact involves establishing the needs of the area and reacting to those needs; in other words, it implies change. Now the ruling political philosophy in a local authority may well be opposed to change. Dearlove,[5] in his study of the Conservative-controlled Borough of Kensington, shows the overwhelming concern of the Council with maintaining existing policies, with resisting change. The Council is described as a 'strong' government, able to ignore demands from the environment and to select only information that lends support to its existing policies. These are very real obstacles to corporate planning and may well frustrate any attempt to introduce such a process into a council subject to permanent control by one political party, particularly where that party is the Conservative Party.

The other principal ideology that has an impact on organisational structures is a belief in participation, whether by elected members or by the public. While a commitment to corporate management is associated with low differentiation and high integration, a commitment to member participation may lead to increased differentiation. On the other hand, it may not lead to more committees, but simply to larger committees. Public participation is dealt with in the next chapter and we will see that political attitudes to public participation vary from one party to another, and the same is true of attitudes to member participation. The Liverpool University study[6] of the attitudes of Merseyside councillors serving on education committees, found that Conservatives regarded their principal role as making policy for education, while Labour members saw their role as protecting the interests and welfare of their constituents. Even more striking is the information that forty per cent of Conservative and thirty per cent of Labour councillors agreed that officers were generally responsible for policy innovation, and only ten per cent thought that individual councillors could make any real contribution to that process. Half the councillors admitted to feeling at a disadvantage in relation to the officers, because the latter had the necessary expertise, information and time required to make policy. The results of this study tend to confirm the analysis of a councillor's functions given in Chapter 4.

Party influences
The formal relationships described above are also influenced by the rather more informal relationships that exist within the authority, particularly the influence of the political parties. Although there are a number of councils where most of the members call themselves Independents, the majority of local authorities – including all the

largest in terms of population and resources – have a majority of party members. Within these authorities, however, party strengths vary considerably. At one extreme there are the authorities where virtually all councillors come from one political party; at the other extreme there are the authorities where three or four political parties share the seats, and there is no overall control. Where the political battle is closely contested, officers will wish to avoid becoming too closely identified with particular policies, as they know that they may well have to work with the opponents of those policies following a change in electoral fortunes. Where one party has permanent control, officers may not feel so inhibited in supporting particular actions. The crucial relationship in most cases is, in any event, that between the political leadership of the majority party and the chief officers. Where a council is organised in party lines, all committee chairmen, and usually vice-chairmen too, will be drawn from the majority party. The leader of the majority party is often formally designated as Leader of the Council and holds the post of Chairman of the Policy and Resources Committee. The various committee chairmen will have been selected by their party colleagues, and can normally count on the support of those colleagues. Thus, even between committee meetings, they can guide the activities of the local authority secure in the knowledge that, should those activities be questioned, they can obtain majority support. Normally, too, the Leader of the Council and other committee chairmen will devote a very considerable proportion of their time to the work of the local authority, indeed for many in the larger councils it is now a full-time occupation. Examples quoted in the press recently include the then Chairman of Nottinghamshire Education Committee who gave up his job in order to devote himself entirely to his work as Chairman. Cooperation and understanding between chairman and chief officer is therefore essential, each relying on the other for support and information. The officer needs consistent and coherent political support for the policies that are being implemented, the chairman needs facts and figures to support his arguments within his own political party group. All major decisions will in fact be taken at a group meeting of the majority party – at which, of course, officers are not present to advise. (It is to overcome this difficulty that some councils have established one-party policy committees.) At group meetings, therefore, chairmen become the major source of information and advice, as they are most closely in touch with the affairs of the authority. For many backbench councillors, their only contacts with chief officers are when they attend committee meetings and when they have an important complaint concerning a department's services: the Chairman is thus the crucial figure as far as the party group is concerned. In addition to this, it must be remembered that the chairman has all the usual powers of that office in relation to committee meetings themselves, including control of the agenda, of the order of debate and a casting vote, if necessary.

Decisions, then, are the product of a very complex network of relationships indeed. A final word of caution: as in any situation involving human relationships, the precise way in which local authorities work depends very much on the personalities and interests of the individuals concerned. There may be one dominant personality on the council. If that councillor's main interest is in a particular area of the council's work, it is not difficult to see that more resources might be given to that area than it might merit in a broader-based judgement. There may be a particular sectional interest on the council: a group of councillors whose livelihood depends upon one specific local industry, for instance. There may be a significant group within the majority party who have a common attachment to a particular geographical area of the authority. Indeed, the representatives of an urban area from different political parties might, on some issues, have more in common with each other than with their party colleagues from rural areas. People do not necessarily behave in exactly the way anticipated by formal organisational structures, nor can these structures ignore the relationships of the people involved in the organisation with people outside the organisation.

6 External relations

Perhaps the most important single factor in local government and politics is the people who are involved. In the last chapter particular emphasis was placed on those who are councillors and those who are local government officers. But there are many other people – pressure groups, civil servants, journalists, government ministers, and not least, the local inhabitants – who are concerned with local government and politics. The style of local politics and the product of local government are determined by the interaction between these various groups of people, by the relationships between them.

Local authorities are subject to many external pressures. Chapter 4, for instance, referred to the influence exerted on party councillors by their political party. The local public also will exert a definite influence on the attitudes of the authority. This will occur in a variety of ways. The authority as a whole (the controlling group and/or the management team, in practice) will act in a manner conditioned by its perception of public opinion. The public can be seen as consumers of the services provided by the council, and as such their views will carry weight. The public can also be seen as the political masters of the council in their capacity as voters. In so far as the dominant motive and objective of the majority group is to maximise their term of office, rather than effect specific policy objectives, then policies which appear to alienate public opinion, and therefore lose votes, will be discarded. Besides having these influences at council level the public also have influence at the level of the individual councillor. The councillor who wishes to retain his seat at the next election will be aware that even a few votes in a ward can make the difference between success and failure, and will therefore normally be extremely responsive to the views expressed by his constituents. This in turn will affect the attitude of the council. Public opinion, then, as perceived by the council and by councillors, will act as a constraint on the activities of the local authority.

Any local authority must also take note of how its decisions affect other authorities, and how their decisions impinge upon its own activities. Every part of the country is subject to a two tier system of local government, with the result that the provision of most major services will in practice require cooperation between the two tiers. Many areas have a third tier to be considered, in the shape of the parish or community councils. Furthermore, local government activity will be affected by the performance of the *ad hoc* authorities, especially those relating to health and to water. Professor J D Stewart refers to the need for 'community planning', where the policy objectives and programmes would be determined by agreement between all the various bodies involved in a given geographical area. Few, if any, parts of the country would claim to have satisfactorily dealt with this problem of integrating decision-taking at the local level. Indeed, it is clear that in practice the provision of local services is a far more complex activity than the usual structure diagram of local authorities would indicate. This is true of all local services, but can perhaps be seen most clearly within the field of planning.

The example of planning

The local authorities may in the first instance find themselves constrained by the work of a regional economic planning council, for example, 'Strategy South East' indicating the areas for major growth, etc. in the South East of England. The county council, e.g. East Sussex County Council, has a responsibility to produce a Structure Plan for its area, which will be concerned with matters such as specifying towns and villages where further residential development will be permitted, indicating areas where development leading to growth of employment will be discouraged, and so on. The County Council must also produce a Transport Policies and Programme document, concerned not only with the road network in the area, but also with the strategy for public transport. This will clearly involve very close cooperation with British Rail and the local bus companies, which will probably be subsidiaries of the National Bus Company, another public corporation. However, local traffic commissioners have the responsibility for licencing bus routes and agreeing fare applications: many county councils are extremely critical of the fact that commissioners' decisions can materially affect the Transport Policies and Programme.

The district councils then have to act within the framework of the County's Structure Plan and Transport Policies and Programme. The districts have the responsibility for local plans, indicating precise land use within a particular settlement, and for development control. This division of responsibility between county and district can give rise to a number of problems; duplication of work, confusion as to what precisely is a 'county matter' and straightforward disagreement over policy, e.g. where a district wishes to grant planning permission for an office development which the county sees as undesirable in terms of the overall Structure Plan. In its development control functions, the district has a statutory obligation to consult the relevant parish council, although it is not bound to agree with the views of the latter. Thus, again, there is the possibility of disagreement between different local authorities.

The planning system therefore involves a number of different authorities when even the most straightforward issue is concerned. But it may be even more complicated. A conurbation, which needs to be planned as a whole, may overlap county boundaries, an application for a housing development may overlap district boundaries. More significantly, decisions by the Regional Water Authority may pre-empt the whole process. No development can take place unless the drainage system is adequate: if the RWA makes no provision in its capital programme for the necessary drainage works, then the schemes of the planning authorities may be frustrated.

Planning is also the local authority function in which public participation is most in evidence. The Skeffington Report in 1969[1] gave a particular impetus to this process. Participation in the preparation of the Structure Plan is a statutory requirement, so too is the public advertisement of planning applications in conservation areas. All planning applications are open to public inspection and public comment. Many councils, furthermore, actively seek the views of the public in the planning process, particularly by consultation with local groups such as the Chamber of Commerce, the Trades Council, and the local Civic Society.

Local groups

This brief discussion of planning gives some indication of the complex nature of relationships, external to the council, in which the local authority is involved when performing its functions. The role of local groups, however, warrants a rather closer examination. This is not the place to attempt a classification of pressure or interest groups. It should be remembered, nevertheless, that pressure groups at the central government level are paralleled by groups at the local government level. Mention has already been made of groups who are likely to be formally consulted by local authorities: the multi-purpose interest group such as the Chamber of Commerce or the Trades Council – who may well have members who serve as Councillors – and the special interest group such as the Conservation Society or the Civic Society, who may well have professional expertise, of which the local authority are pleased to take advantage. Other permanent groups are concerned with defending or promoting the interests of a particular geographical area, such as a local Residents' Association; they are likely to exert influence mainly through the ward councillor(s). Two further types of permanent group are the defensive, such as the Ratepayers' Association, and the promotional, such as the Confederation for the Advancement of State Education: these will tend to operate at the level of public opinion and affect council policies in the way indicated at the beginning of this chapter. Most noticeable at the local level are the temporary groups, usually formed as a protective measure, to protest about the proposed site for a refuse tip, or the proposed route for a new road. Besides the more conventional methods of trying to exert influence, such groups will make full use of protest marches, demonstrations, and other forms of direct action.

The attitudes of councillors, and councils, to pressure groups can be predicted to some extent by the political composition of the council. In the first place, councillors may simply not know of the existence of groups. In the Liverpool University study of the politics of education on Merseyside[2] – and education is an area renowned for the number of groups that operate, their vociferousness, and their knowledge of the system – eighty per cent of Conservative councillors said that they were unaware of any groups that might be operating in their constituency; Labour councillors seemed to be slightly more aware of the existence of such groups, but to have little active contact. However, while Labour members welcomed the contribution that groups could make to policy-making, Conservative members were generally unsympathetic as they saw policy-making as the exclusive responsibility of the elected member. Dearlove's study in Kensington[3] confirms the conclusion that Conservative councillors tend, if possible, to ignore groups unless they are cooperative, in the sense of lending support to existing policies. In general, groups are going to be successful only if their objectives fit fairly well with the objectives and philosophy of the local majority party. They will be resisted if councillors imagine that groups are aiming to embarrass elected representatives and to usurp the councillor's role.

The experience of planning authorities since 1968 suggests that the attempt at increased public participation has resulted in continuous discussions with other public bodies, with large firms, and with 'permanent' groups of status; in long comments from some groups and individuals – some of these comments being relevant, some not, some detailed, some very broad; and in considerable cost in terms both of money and manpower. It is open to discussion whether this process can be described as more democratic government than a system without participation. Is democracy more than rule by elected politicians? Does it involve continuous public involvement? Are majority views expressed in public participation exercises, or only the views of an articulate and interested minority? If the latter, does it matter? Does participation lead to more conflict, or does it actually reduce conflict, as the public become more aware of the reasons for certain actions and the constraints facing the local authority?

The media
Pressure groups and individual members of the public who are trying to participate in or influence the decisions of the local authority will look to the mass media to publicise their causes. Although television plays a part, particularly in the metropolitan areas, the mass media in its coverage of local government tends to mean the local press. The relationship between local authorities and the press has always been an uncomfortable one. Local authorities accuse the press of sensationalism and distortion, while the press

accuse local authorities of unnecessary secrecy. In fact, each needs the other: local authorities need the press to inform the public of what is being done in their name or is intended to be done; the press need the news of major events and decisions affecting their readers.

Surprisingly, many local newspapers do not give an adequate coverage of local council affairs – despite the direct influence the council has on the standard and style of living of the newspapers' readers. In a study of six newspapers covering Merseyside[4], with a combined circulation of well over half-a-million, the researchers found that only some four per cent of the space was devoted to political matters. This compared with forty per cent given over to advertisements, fifteen per cent to sport and three per cent to births, marriages and deaths. Even the four per cent included a substantial proportion given over to snippets of news which did little to help readers gain an impression of the issues being resolved on their behalf. However, the blame for this state of affairs cannot be allocated to the press alone. Until the last decade, many local authorities managed to obscure their activities in a mixture of secrecy and impenetrable jargon. In recent years, though, much has been done to lift the 'murky cloak' from the activities of local authorities. Since 1974 all committee, as well as council, meetings are required to be open to press and public. It should be noted, however, that the committee or council can resolve to exclude the press and public on the grounds of 'the confidential nature of the business to be transacted'; sub-committees do not have to be open; and some observers have noted a growth in the use of sub-committees since 1974. The relationship with the press inevitably varies from one authority to another. At one extreme, the press are excluded from as much as possible; at the other, as in some London Boroughs, they are admitted even to the meetings of the majority group where the real decisions are made. The reactions of the newspapers to the decisions of the council are affected by the degree of cooperation they receive in their attempts to cover the activities of the council. It should never be forgotten, however, that most local newspapers have a political bias and their editorial policy should be seen in that context.

Parliament

The major external constraint on local authorities is the simple fact that, like other participants in the British political system, they are subordinate to the will of Parliament. They have no freedom and no rights other than those which Parliament chooses to give them. This applies to all levels of local authority, from the smallest parish or community to the largest metropolitan county; indeed, within the context of the British constitutional system, the same would undoubtedly be true of any regional, provincial, or 'national' unit of government. This latter point was clearly illustrated by the ability of the United Kingdom Government to impose direct rule on Northern Ireland at the expense of Stormont.

Any action of a local council, then, must have statutory authority; that is, the council must be able to point to an Act of Parliament which explicitly grants it the power to act in that particular way. If the local authority cannot justify its actions by reference to the law, it may be said to be acting *ultra vires* – beyond its powers – and may be challenged in the courts or at audit time. The only exception to this restriction on local authorities is that any council may spend, each year, a sum up to the product of a 2p rate on anything that it considers to be 'in the general interests of the inhabitants, or some of the inhabitants, of the area'. Even here, a special resolution of the council is required; nor can it use this provision to provide a service which Parliament has forbidden local authorities to provide. For example, the Education (Milk) Act of 1971 specifically forbids local education authorities to provide free milk for schoolchildren between seven and eleven years old.

Parliament passes legislation of various kinds affecting local authorities. The vast majority of Acts of Parliament concerning local authorities are in fact Private Acts, sponsored by individual local authorities themselves. As explained above, a local authority cannot undertake any action unless there exists statutory authorisation. If it wishes to provide a service for which there is no such statutory authority, the simplest course is to promote a Private Bill in Parliament. Examples of such Bills in recent years include the GLC's (unsuccessful) attempt to obtain powers to run a lottery as a means of obtaining additional revenue. That particular Bill was opposed by the Government and therefore failed to obtain Parliamentary approval; most Private Bills, however, are uncontroversial and experience a relatively untroubled passage into law. Indeed most are concerned with fairly technical matters such as methods of financing major schemes – such as a marina, or a swing bridge – and obtaining powers for the compulsory purchase of land necessary for such schemes.

Parliament also passes legislation affecting all local authorities. Occasionally, such legislation may take the form of Bills introduced by Private Members: an example from recent years being the Chronically Sick and Disabled Persons Act. More usually, however, it will be in the form of Bills introduced by the Government itself, which can range from the most fundamental kind of measure such as the Local Government Act 1972, to the rather more trivial such as the Rural Water Supplies and Sewerage Act 1971. A useful classification of general Acts is to divide them into those that are obligatory and those that are permissive. Obligatory Acts are those that place a duty upon a local authority: failure to comply may lead to ministerial intervention or to a court action. Thus, all local education authorities have a duty to provide schooling for those aged between five and sixteen years. Permissive Acts simply give local authorities the power to perform a certain service, if they so wish. For example, the Transport Act allows local authorities to introduce concessionary bus fare schemes, but they are not compelled to do so.

Parliament, then, is a constraint on the actions of local authorities; Parliament gives powers and may take them away. This supremacy of Parliament can be quoted as a principal feature of the British constitution, of a unitary system of government. It would be misleading, however, to deduce from this that Members of Parliament are the controllers of local government. An examination of power relationships within the House of Commons is outside the scope of this book, but the evidence would tend to suggest that government ministers are able to dominate the House of Commons. If they oppose a Private Bill or a Private Member's Bill, it will not pass: they must consent to any proposals involving public expenditure – as virtually all legislation in the local government field must. Parliamentary control of local government may therefore be seen as another means of ministerial control.

The courts
Local authorities, then, find themselves subject to a complex network of legislation. It follows from this that their actions or

inaction may be challenged in the courts. They are of course sometimes involved in cases concerning contract or tort, as any other legal personality might be, but because of the range of legislation that applies to local government alone, there is a considerable body of local government case law. A local authority resident may, for instance, seek a declaration from the High Court that the local authority is acting *ultra vires*, as was held to be the case with Birmingham's concessionary bus fares scheme in 1954. Alternatively, the High Court may issue an order of prohibition, ordering an authority to cease an action; an order of mandamus, ordering an authority to perform a duty laid upon them by the law; or an order of certiorari, requiring an authority to review a decision taken by them when acting in a quasi-judicial manner, e.g. granting a licence. Judicial control of local authorities, however, cannot be seen as an effective general control in that it is marginal, in the true sense of that word; it is haphazard, since it depends on the interest, resources and stamina of individual members of the electorate; and it is partial, in that the courts are usually involved only where the law is unclear. Nevertheless, it can be a political weapon, in the sense that cases may well be initiated by those who are political opponents of the party controlling the local council. An example would be the Enfield school case in 1967 when, although the court was merely asked to determine the correctness of the procedures followed by the local authority, the intention of the plaintiffs was to obstruct and, if possible, prevent the local authority from going ahead with its scheme for comprehensive schools in the area. An additional point to notice is that, in one sense at least, judicial control can be seen as an extension of ministerial control. The courts are, after all, the agents for ensuring that the laws, the bulk of which have been sponsored by the government, are enforced. Furthermore, if a minister dislikes the courts' interpretation of the law, he is in a position to remove misunderstanding by introducing amending legislation into Parliament and by using his majority to pass it. For instance, following the Birmingham case mentioned above, the law was altered to allow those authorities operating concessionary fare schemes to continue to do so.

Ministers

It could be argued therefore that both parliamentary and judicial control are, in part, aspects of ministerial control. However, ministers have a much more direct influence over the actions of local authorities through the administrative controls exercised by their government departments. A number of government departments are involved in this way with the local authorities, the principal ones being the Department of the Environment, the Scottish Office, the Welsh Office, the Department of Education and Science, and the Department of Health and Social Security. The relationship between local authorities and central government departments is sometimes likened to a partnership, sometimes to a master-servant relationship. Both descriptions contain an element of truth, and neither generalisation would be adequate on its own, for the relationship varies from service to service, some being subject to greater central control than others. Greater control is normally exercised over those local government activities which are most expensive, both in terms of current and capital expenditure. Central government here sees control of local government as merely one aspect of the overall control of public expenditure, which in turn is largely determined by decisions concerning the direction of the national economy as a whole. The other major reason for greater central control of some services than of others is political sensitivity. Certain services – education and housing, for instance, rather than refuse disposal and playing fields – are major issues in national politics; ministers will wish to claim political credit for achievements and will be attacked for failures in these areas. Inevitably, therefore, they will wish to have ways of controlling local authority activity, for it is the local authorities who in the last resort are the providing authorities: it is they who must act.

In some instances Parliament has given a minister very general powers over local authorities. In the field of education, for instance, the 1944 Act places the duty of providing schooling on the local authorities 'under the general guidance' of the Minister. Interpreted widely, this would seem to give the Minister freedom to intervene on almost any matter if he so chooses. In practice ministers have interpreted the phrase as merely giving them the right to establish national principles in educational policy. They have used the methods described below to attempt to ensure that those principles are observed at the local level.

In certain cases ministers possess default powers. This means that if the Minister considers a local authority is not performing a statutory duty, he can transfer responsibility for the service concerned from the council to a commissioner appointed by himself and the local authority will have to meet the costs involved. An example occurred in Coventry in relation to Civil Defence in 1954. Much the best known cases, however, arose out of the 1972 Housing Finance Act. This Act required local housing authorities to increase the rents payable by council tenants by a specified sum each year, and at the same time to introduce a rent rebate scheme. The Act was bitterly criticised by many local authorities, councillors often pointing out that they had been elected on platforms specifically opposing rent increases. A classic problem of democracy was thus in issue. Should the views of those elected locally or of those elected nationally prevail? The legal position was quite clear, in that Parliament is sovereign. Nevertheless, a number of local authorities, prominent among which was Clay Cross Urban District Council in Derbyshire, refused to implement the Act. At Clay Cross, and in one or two other instances, the Minister then installed a Housing Commissioner. The refusal of the Clay Cross Council to cooperate in any way with the Commissioner – no office space, no use of staff, no access to records – illustrated how difficult it could be for central government to get its own way when confronted by a really recalcitrant local authority. The whole saga was, perhaps fortunately, cut short by the disappearance of the Clay Cross Council under local government reorganisation in April 1974.

Normally, however, ministers' powers of influence over local authorities are such that they do not have to resort to such drastic action as installing commissioners, even where they have the power to do so. In many fields local authorities need ministerial approval of their schemes: of a compulsory purchase order, of proposed byelaws, of a county's structure plan, of proposals for the reorganisation of secondary education. Ministers can and do withhold their approval when schemes violate national policy. For instance, between 1970 and 1974 the Conservative Secretary of State for Education and Science refused approval for a number of schemes submitted by local authorities for the reorganisation of secondary education along comprehensive lines.

Government departments from time to time issue circulars, bulletins and other documents which may be merely advisory or may require action. For instance in 1974 the Labour Secretary of State for Education required all local authorities, that had not already done so, to submit schemes for comprehensive reorganisation. What are the consequences of failure to comply with such a request or directive? In the long-term, legislation may result, compelling authorities to act in a particular way. In the short-term, penalties are likely to be financial. In the first place, local authorities are heavily dependent on central government financial assistance. In the field of housing, for instance, central government subsidy to local authorities is very considerable: it was the threat of having these subsidies withdrawn that brought many councils into line over the 1972 Housing Finance Act. Secondly, as explained in the section on finance, local authorities cannot borrow money for capital schemes without ministerial approval. This loan sanction procedure applies in particular detail to key sector projects, which include education and housing. Thus a minister who wishes to advance comprehensive education could refuse loan sanction for all secondary school projects which do not form part of a comprehensive scheme. In these circumstances local authorities are going to find it expedient, at the very least, to comply with central government policy.

Besides the controls already outlined, there are still many others. The short list of candidates for appointment as Director of Social Services has to be approved by the Minister; a Chief Constable cannot be dismissed without ministerial consent; schemes for housebuilding, if they are to receive loan sanction, must come within the Ministry's 'cost yardstick'; when a design for a new school is submitted for loan sanction, the detailed plans are checked by the Ministry's architects. This last example can be used to illustrate the case made by many in local government that central controls are unnecessary and can be positively harmful. Such controls imply a lack of faith in the ability and competence of local authorities and their staff, and they involve considerable delay and time-wasting, which in the long run will probably involve local authorities in increased costs. The situation does of course arise where plans drawn up by local authorities' architects are being vetted by less well qualified and less experienced ministry staff.

From time to time, too, central government is tempted to extend its range of controls. In 1973 for instance the government insisted on the monitoring of rates. Local authorities were required to submit their rate budgets for 1973-1974 to the Ministry. If the Ministry considered that the percentage increase over the previous year was too large, they requested the local authority to cut a specified sum from their estimates. The reactions of local authorities varied. Some cut their estimates as requested, others ignored the request – for request was all that it could be, since the Government has no statutory control over rate levels. To some extent, local reaction was a function of the political complexion of the council: Conservative local authorities tended to comply with the wishes of the Conservative government, while Labour local authorities tended not to. The experiment has not so far been repeated.

Attitudes to control

To some extent, then, the degree of central control can be related to willingness on the part of the local authority to allow itself to be controlled. This applies especially in the type of case illustrated above, where central government is limited to making a request. The responsiveness of the local authority may well depend on its political complexion, as compared with that of the national government, and the intensity or predominance of party politics within the authority. Another determining factor may be the attitude and self-confidence of the council's officers. There are those who always interpret government requests as directives, and, if uncertain of the interpretation of a statute or a circular, will write or telephone the relevant ministry official and accept his advice as to the interpretation. There are also those who are prepared to prefer their own counsels to those of the civil servants. Usually, too, the larger the local authority, the less likely it is to bow to central government pressure. Manchester, Birmingham, Sheffield – authorities such as these know that central government requires their assistance and cooperation if its policies in education, social services and housing are to be successful; they play a major part in the activities of the local authority associations, with which the government will consult and negotiate; their leaders are usually influential in their political parties at national level, and thus cannot be over-ruled or ignored. The small district council, however, lacks these advantages and may therefore find it more politic to comply with central requests.

The attitude of the political parties at national level towards central control is an interesting study in itself. Politicians of all parties, especially when in opposition, call for greater freedom of action for local government. So too have committees and Royal commissions over the years since 1945. Certainly some controls have been lifted. Fewer appointments are subject to control than was the case before the 1972 Act, for example, and the delaying effects of others have been ameliorated. For instance, the 1968 provision that certain planning appeals may be determined by the Minister's Inspector himself. Nevertheless, particularly where finance is concerned and finance is crucial, central control is still very tight.

The schizophrenic attitude of national politicians towards central control can be illustrated by the difference between their words in opposition and their actions in government. Thus, during the period 1964-1970, the Conservative Opposition attacked the Government's comprehensive schools policy on the grounds that it denied freedom of choice to local education authorities. However, the Conservative Government between 1970 and 1974 rejected a number of local authority schemes for comprehensive schools. This suggests that the objection was not in fact to the infringement of local authority freedom but to the Labour comprehensive policy itself. Similarly, the Labour Opposition attacked the 1972 Housing Finance Act on the grounds that it removed the right to fix council rents as they saw fit from local authorities. When in Government after 1974, however, Labour repealed the Housing Finance Act, and they included in the new Act a power for the Minister to issue an Order limiting the amount of rent increases. This suggests that the objection was not in fact to the infringement of local authority freedom but to the Conservative rents policy itself. Political realities emerge more clearly from actions than from words.

Audit

Before leaving the topic of formal external controls on the actions of local authorities, there are two other institutions that must be mentioned: District Audit and the Commission for Local Administration. When a local authority has closed its accounts for a given financial year those accounts must be submitted to audit. Although, strictly speaking, the District Audit service is not part of the Department of the Environment, it is responsible to the Secretary of State for the Environment. District auditors fulfil a task at the local level that is in many ways similar to the work of the Comptroller and Auditor-General advising the Public Accounts Committee at national level. The task of the auditor is to ensure that the accounts have been drawn up in the prescribed manner, and that there has been no unauthorised expenditure. It is open to any ratepayer to challenge an item in the accounts at audit time. 'Unauthorised' expenditure refers to any expenditure undertaken on a service that appears to be *ultra vires*. Such cases are now few and far between, although Clay Cross UDC between 1972 and 1974 again serves as an example. Indeed, at the time of writing in 1976, the District Auditor is still considering items in that Council's accounts referring to overspending in making payments to workers, employing more staff than was necessary and borrowing money for which no provision was made for interest.

The Minister may, as with the Housing Account at Clay Cross, order an extraordinary audit to take place apart from the normal audit timetable. If the auditor considers that certain expenditure is unauthorised, he may apply to the court for a declaration to that effect. Normally this has meant that those councillors whose votes led to the unauthorised expenditure will have to find the money from their own pockets. The Clay Cross councillors were originally surcharged £7,000, but the final figure is likely to be at least £67,000. The type of case just referred to, however, forms a very small part of the everyday work of the District Auditor service. In the main the service is now really concerned with conducting an efficiency audit and providing advice to local authorities. The auditor might suggest to a local authority, for instance, that its method of providing a particular service appears unduly costly, and might draw its attention to the experience and practice of other authorities who are providing a similar service rather more economically.

Local Ombudsmen

Commissioners for Local Administration – or, as they tend to be known, Local Ombudsmen – have been in existence only since 1974. Each commissioner is responsible for one region of the country, and has the task of investigating complaints of maladministration made against local authorities in that region. By contrast with the arrangements for the Parliamentary Commissioner for Administration, it is possible for a member of the public to send a complaint directly to the local commissioner, if he has not received a satisfactory reply from the local authority, although it is anticipated that local authorities would conduct their own enquiries into complaints in the first instance. An example of the type of complaint that might be referred to a local commissioner is unreasonable delay in granting planning permission. In its first year, the Commission for Local Administration received 473 complaints, of which 347 were in fact held to be outside its terms of reference. Of the first ten cases investigated, maladministration was found in six. The Commission has no powers to force a local authority to behave in a particular way: its weapon is publicity. Like the Parliamentary commissioner, the local commissioners can perhaps best be seen, not so much as a type of central control, but as a means of satisfying public grievances: an independent investigation does much to remove a sense of injustice even if it does not produce a favourable result for the complainant.

Local authorities, then, have to take note of a whole range of external constraints. The relationships with the various institutions and individuals mentioned in this chapter have an effect both on the methods of operation of the local authority and the type of decisions that they take.

When these external relationships are added to the internal relationships, the complex nature of local government and politics becomes apparent. Institutional arrangements may alter as the years go by, but the basic political truth remains that institutions are designed to serve political objectives. Individuals and groups have their own ideas of the kind of society they wish to see at local or national level. Institutions should provide a means for the expression of these ideas, for the resolution of conflicts between competing ideas, and for the implementation of decisions resulting from such resolutions. Local government is all too often examined in an entirely institutional manner – it is essential to remember that institutions are only a means to the end.

Notes and References

Chapter 1 The structure of local government

1. Particularly important are:
   The Committee on the Management of Local Government (The Maud Report): Appointed 1964, reported 1967.
   The Royal Commission on Local Government in England (The Redcliffe-Maud Report): Appointed 1966, reported 1969.
   The Royal Commission on Local Government in Scotland (The Wheatley Report): Appointed 1966, reported 1969.
2. Redcliffe-Maud Report: Volume 1, Paragraph 6.
3. G.C. Broderick, *Local Government and Taxation*, 1885, quoted in the Redcliffe-Maud Report, Volume III, Paragraph 11.
4. The Seebohm Report, Paragraph 388.
5. Redcliffe-Maud Report, Paragraph 92.
6. *The Reform of Local Government in Wales* (HMSO, 1971.)
7. Appendix to AMA Policy Committee report 5/1974.

Chapter 2 Regionalism and nationalism

1. Royal Commission on the Constitution, Attitude Survey, page 58.
2. Royal Commission on the Constitution, page 155, paragraph 515.
3. Ibid., paragraph 517.
4. Page 129.
5. Paragraph 493.
6. Paragraph 13.

Chapter 3 Finance

1. Water authorities also issue precepts to the district councils for water and sewerage services. Some water authorities, however, are now contemplating collecting their rate income directly from ratepayers.

2. There exists considerable confusion as to the proportion of local authority expenditure provided by the central government. It is quite usual to come across statements such as 'Central government provides about two-thirds of local government's spending'. This error arises as a result of a misunderstanding of the nature of government assistance. In 1976-1977 aggregate exchequer assistance was 65.5 per cent of local authority *relevant* expenditure. Relevant expenditure, however, excludes certain local authority expenditure, and refers also to expenditure net of income such as fees, charges, etc. For a full discussion of these points, see A. Crispin, Local Government Finance: Assessing the Central Government's Contribution, *Public Administration*, Spring 1976.
3. There is nevertheless some evidence that the political complexion of the local authority does affect the amount of its expenditure. In particular it appears that Labour Councils tend to spend more than other local authorities. See D.N. King, Why do Local Authority Rate Poundages Differ?, *Public Administration*, Summer 1973.
4. N. Topham, A Case for Abolishing RSG, *Local Government Chronicle*, 10 October 1975.

Chapter 4 Polls and politicians

1. See, for example, Iain McLean, *Elections*, in this series.
2. C.R. Bagley, Does Candidates' Position on the Ballot Paper Influence Voters' Choice?, *Parliamentary Affairs*, Spring 1966.
3. For a discussion of the objectives of the political parties, see other titles in this series, especially L.J. McFarlane, *Issues in British Politics since 1945*.
4. A description of party group activity is contained in H.V. Wiseman, *Local Government at Work* (Routledge and Kegan Paul, 1967.)
5. H. Morrison, quoted in B. Donoughue and Jones, *Herbert Morrison, Portrait of a Politician* (Weidenfeld and Nicolson, 1973.)
6. M. Kogan and W. Van Der Eyken, *County Hall* (Penguin, 1973.)
7. *The New Local Authorities: Management and Structure* (The Bains Report) (HMSO, 1972.)

Chapter 5 Internal relations

1. For more detailed information on 'City Managers' and many of the other developments mentioned in this chapter, see *Local Government Chronicle* which has carried articles on these topics during most weeks since 1967. More specifically, see J. Elliott, The Harris Experiment in Newcastle-upon-Tyne, *Public Administration*, Summer 1971.

2. Quoted in Horace Keast, Management Structures Reviewed, *Local Government Chronicle*, 20 June 1975.
3. Bains, page 52.
4. For a fuller examination of these concepts, and their application to existing local authorities, see R. Greenwood, C.R. Hinings and S. Ranson, Contingency Theory and the Organisation of Local Authorities, *Public Administration*, Spring and Summer 1975. Greenwood, Hinings and Ranson are members of the Institute of Local Government Studies (INLOGOV) at the University of Birmingham. The INLOGOV survey referred to in this chapter is the research on which their article quoted is based.
5. J. Dearlove, *The Politics of Policy in Local Government* (Cambridge University Press, 1973.)
6. *Politics of Urban Education,* Department of Political Theory and Institutions, University of Liverpool, 1973.

Chapter 6 External relations

1. *People and Planning – Report of the Committee on Public Participation in Planning* (HMSO, 1969.)
2. *Politics of Urban Education*, op. cit.
3. J. Dearlove, op. cit.
4. H. Cox and D. Morgan, *City Politics and the Press – Journalists and the Governing of Merseyside* (Cambridge University Press, 1974.)

Bibliography

Chapter 1 **The Structure of local government**

J. Brand, *Local Government Reform in England, 1888-1974* Croom Helm, 1975.

Lord Redcliffe-Maud and Bruce Wood, *English Local Government Reformed* Oxford University Press, 1974.

J. Redlich and F.W. Hirst, *History of Local Government* Macmillan, 1958.

L.J. Sharpe, 'Theories and Values of Local Government' in R.A. Chapman and A. Dunsire (eds.) *Style and Administration* Allen and Unwin, 1971.

K.B. Smellie, *A History of Local Government* Allen and Unwin, 1968.

W. Thornhill (ed.), *The Growth and Reform of English Local Government* Weidenfeld and Nicolson, 1971.

H.V. Wiseman, *Local Government in England, 1958-1969* Routledge and Kegan Paul, 1970.

Reference should also be made to the various Government Reports listed in Note 1 to this chapter.

Chapter 2 **Regionalism and nationalism**

J.C. Banks, *Federal Britain* Harrap, 1971.

W. Hampton, *Democracy and Community: a study of Politics in Sheffield* Oxford University Press, 1970.

D. Heald, *Making Devolution Work* Fabian Society, 1976.

D.M. Hill, *Democratic Theory and Local Government* Allen and Unwin, 1974.

J.P. Mackintosh, *The Devolution of Power* Penguin, 1968.

W. Thornhill, *The Case for Regional Reform* Nelson, 1972.

The Royal Commission on the Constitution (The Kilbrandon Report) HMSO, 1973.

Devolution within the United Kingdom: Some Alternatives for Discussion HMSO, 1974.

Our Changing Democracy: Devolution to Scotland and Wales HMSO, 1975.

Scotland and Wales Bill HMSO, 1976.
Devolution and Regional Government in England Labour Party, 1975.

Chapter 3 **Finance**
N.P. Hepworth, *The Finance of Local Government* Allen and Unwin, 1970.
A.H. Marshall, *New Revenues for Local Government* Fabian Society, 1972.
A.H. Marshall, *Financial Management in Local Government* Allen and Unwin, 1974.
H.V. Wiseman, *Local Government at Work* Routledge and Kegan Paul, 1967.
The Future Shape of Local Government Finance HMSO, 1971.
Local Government Finance – Report of the Committee of Inquiry (The Layfield Report) HMSO, 1976.

Chapter 4 **Polls and politicians**
J.G. Bulpitt, *Party Politics in English Local Government* Longmans, 1967.
I. Gowans, 'The role and power of political parties in local government' in J.D. Lees and R. Kimber (eds.), *Political Parties in Modern Britain* Routledge and Kegan Paul, 1972.
W. Hampton, *Democracy and Community: a study of Politics in Sheffield* Oxford University Press, 1970.
J.M. Lee, *Social Leaders and Public Persons* Oxford University Press, 1963.
I. McLean, *Elections* Longman, 1976.
P.G.J. Pulzer, *Political Representation and Elections in Britain* Allen and Unwin, 1967.
A. Rees and T. Smith, *Town Councillors* Acton Society Trust, 1964.
M. Stewart, *Unpaid Public Service* Fabian Society, 1964.
Management of Local Government (The Maud Report) HMSO, 1967: especially Volume II.

Chapter 5 **Internal relations**
R. Buxton, *Local Government* 2nd Edition, Penguin, 1973.
I. Hill, *Corporate Planning* Paisley College of Technology, 1973.
M. Kogan and W. Van Der Eyken, *County Hall* Penguin, 1973.
B.J. Ripley, *Administration in Local Authorities* Butterworths, 1970.
Staffing of Local Government (The Mallaby Report) HMSO, 1967.
Management of Local Government (The Maud Report) HMSO, 1967.
Royal Commission on Local Government in England (The Redcliffe-Maud Report) HMSO, 1969.
The New Local Authorities: Management and Structure (The Bains Report) HMSO, 1972.

Chapter 6 **External relations**

R. Burke, *The Murky Cloak* Charles Knight & Co., 1970.

C.A. Cross, *Principles of Local Government Law* 5th edition, Sweet and Maxwell, 1974.

J.A.G. Griffith, *Central Departments and Local Authorities* Allen and Unwin, 1966.

G.M. Higgins and J.J. Richardson, *Political Participation* The Politics Association, 1976.

D.M. Hill, *Participating in Local Affairs* Penguin, 1970.

People and Planning: Report of the Committee on Public Participation in Planning (The Skeffington Report) HMSO, 1969.

Index